SUBJECTIVITY AND PARADOX

SUBJECTIVITY
AND
PARADOX

By

J. HEYWOOD THOMAS

OXFORD
BASIL BLACKWELL
1957

First printed February, 1957

PRINTED IN GREAT BRITAIN
BY A. T. BROOME AND SON, ST. CLEMENT'S OXFORD.
AND BOUND BY THE KEMP HALL BINDERY, OXFORD

UXORI MATRIQUE
AMATISSIMIS
AUCTORIS LIBRIQUE
PROGENITORIBUS

CONTENTS

PREFACE

There have been so many books written on Kierkegaard in recent years that the publication of yet another one may need some sort of apology. Yet anyone who wishes to make a serious study of him will soon find that the literature available in English is for the most part of an introductory nature. This book has been written because I am sure that the time has come when introductions are no longer useful. It attempts to illustrate Kierkegaard's contribution to the Philosophy of Religion by a detailed examination of two of his dominant concepts. I began my work in Cambridge in 1950, and I would like here to acknowledge my debt to the Rev. Prof. H. H. Farmer who guided my steps in those first years. Cambridge in fact gave me what I regard as the most useful way of interpreting Kierkegaard—that is the attempt to translate his thought by means of the linguistic technique. Hence I asked myself two questions : firstly, What in fact was it that Kierkegaard wanted to say? and secondly, is what he wanted to say meaningful and significant now? In New York I had the privilege of discussing Kierkegaard with Prof. Paul Tillich. Not least because his interpretation of Kierkegaard was different from mine, Tillich contributed much to my thinking. I am grateful to him.

I must also acknowledge my indebtedness to the following : The Swenson-Kierkegaard Memorial Fellowship Committee encouraged me in my work by electing me to the Fellowship for 1954. And now that the book is published the University of Wales Press has very generously made a grant to defray part of the cost of its production. To the publishers, however, my main thanks are due for their willingness to make possible this memorial to Søren Kierkegaard.

It would be impossible for me to indicate how much I am indebted to particular works on Kierkegaard. Yet I must say— what is perhaps obvious—that I am greatly indebted to the many scholars who have worked in this rich field. Clearly one cannot afford to neglect such works as Lowrie's and Geismar's great books—to mention but two of the truly great Kierkegaard

scholars. I am sorry I was not able to read Prof. James Collins'
valuable book, *The Mind of Kierkegaard*, which did not appear until
after my book was finished.

I am obliged to the following publishers for permission to
make the quotations which appear in the book : The Oxford
University Press, The Cambridge University Press, Faber and
Faber Ltd., and The Epworth Press.

The Editor of the *Review of Religion* has kindly allowed me
to use in Chapter 4 material which had appeared as an article in
his journal.

J. HEYWOOD THOMAS.

CHAPTER I

INTRODUCTION

A century ago a man died in Copenhagen whose life had been exhausted in a struggle with official Christianity. Søren Aabye Kierkegaard had been born in the ' harbour of merchandise ' in 1813. He was not a heretic—neither was he a fool. Indeed it is now common knowledge that he was a man of great genius, an able philosopher, a powerful theologian and an earnest disciple of New Testament Christianity.

Kierkegaard, whose name is to-day so familiar to every reader of philosophy and theology, was practically unknown to the English-speaking world until about 1910. The first reference to him in English is probably to be found in the account a young Scotsman gave of his travels in Denmark. Andrew Hamilton describes him thus :

> ' . . . a man whom it is impossible to omit in any account of Denmark, but whose place it might be more difficult to fix . . . . But as his works have, at all events for the most part, a religious tendency, he may find a place among the theologians. He is a philosophical Christian writer, evermore dwelling, one might almost say harping, on the theme of the human heart. There is no Danish writer more in earnest than he, yet there is no one in whose way stand more things to prevent his becoming popular. He writes at times with an exaggerated display of logic that disgusts the public. All very well if he were not a popular writer, but it is for this that he intends himself.'[1]

Some forty years elapse before we find another direct reference to Kierkegaard in an article on Ibsen published in 1899 :

> ' . . . in his poem *Brand* Ibsen has . . . clothed in dramatic drapery some of the tenets propounded in the neglected works of Kirkegaard (*sic*) . . . For the religious philosophy of this Danish thinker contained none of the usual narcotics

---

[1] Andrew Hamilton, *Sixteen Months in the Danish Isles*, Richard Bentley, London, 1852, vol. II, pp. 268–9.

of philosophy or the opiates of religion. Truth, for Kierkegaard, lies in Subjectivity alone. "Subjectiviteten, Inderilghe-
den er Sandheden." [1]

There was no study of Kierkegaard's work in English until
Francis Fulford, one-time Scholar of Jesus College, Cambridge,
Rector of Turney, published his monograph in Cambridge in
1911. Then in 1935 John A. Bain's work, *Søren Kierkegaard His
Life and Religious Teaching* was published in London. Both are
interesting and good enough as far as they go, but neither can be
called a scholarly exposition or a good criticism of Kierkegaard's
work. Lowrie's great work, published in 1938, provided English
readers with the first authoritative biography of Kierkegaard
and an enthusiastic description of what he stood for and had
achieved. At the same time Lowrie put all English readers under
great obligation by his able translations of so many of Kierkegaard's writings. This gradual growth of English familiarity
with Kierkegaard has now reached a strange climax in that so
many people know him, as it were by reputation, and so few
take the trouble to find out for themselves what he says. A spate
of popular works upon him continues to issue from the press,
works which do not clarify the situation overmuch ; and so long
as the present interest in Kierkegaard produces only this kind of
work we shall be neglecting the task of seriously taking stock of
what Kierkegaard has contributed—whether it be to philosophy
or to theology, or again to the border-line study of the philosophy
of religion.

That he has made a definite contribution to philosophy is
admitted by historians of philosophy. For instance, Brock says :

' I am inclined to believe that, if the history of the
philosophy of Christianity were to be written, his (i.e.
Kierkegaard's) interpretation would be ranked among the
few great efforts to conceive Christianity as it originally was,
an attempt made formerly by Augustine and by Luther.
But there is this difference, that Kierkegaard undertook this
task in the middle of the 19th Century when the secularisa-
tion of the European peoples was far advanced, that, unlike

[1] M. A. Stobart, ' New Lights in Ibsen's " Brand ",' *The Fortnightly Review*
New Series, vol. LXVI, pp. 227–8. I am indebted to Prof. Downs, Master of
Christ's College, Cambridge, for this reference.

Luther, he aimed at an ultimate philosophical clarification.
. . .'[1]

It becomes necessary then for us to see exactly what Kierkegaard
has achieved in terms of philosophical clarification. This is
precisely what we hope to do by an examination of a single
theme in his work. The danger of such a procedure is to deal
with something which is of only academic interest, but we believe
that we have avoided this danger inasmuch as we have chosen
what may with justice be regarded as the most important of
Kierkegaard's categories. Although his work covered a multitude
of themes, Kierkegaard himself admits that there was one dominant theme in all his work. In the *Point of View* he says that he
was at all periods of his authorship a religious writer.[2] He sought
to answer the question : What does it mean for me to become a
Christian? Thus Kierkegaard's work might almost be said to be
a *locus classicus* for studying the main problem of philosophy of
religion, which is that of understanding the nature of religious
faith. He was himself an example of what as a philosopher he
sought to analyse and describe. The task he has set himself was
that of protesting against the dreadful misinterpretation of
Christianity both by the speculative philosopher and the facile
' Christian '. Whilst scholars have admitted the religious inspiration of Kierkegaard's work they have not always been in agreement about the interpretation of his work in the light of this fact.
For instance, Bishop Bohlin is so conscious of the religious
character of Kierkegaard's work that he would distinguish sharply
between his piety and his intellectual expression of it, his philosophy of religion, and attaches value only to the former.[3]

Lowrie also emphasises the religious nature of Kierkegaard's
work, though he would probably not agree with Bohlin's interpretation of it. Speaking of the likeness between Kierkegaard
and Pascal and Nietzsche he insists that the likeness to the latter
is a surprising likeness between the Christian and ' the Anti-
christ ' and is not at all as positive a likeness as that between
Kierkegaard and Dostoievsky.[4] Prof. Reidar Thomte ends his

---

[1] Brock, *Contemporary German Philosophy*, Cambridge, 1935, pp. 76–7.
[2] *The Point of View for my work as an author*, p. 5 f.
[3] Bohlin, *Kierkegaard's Dogmatiska Åskådning*, Stockholm, 1925.
[4] Lowrie, *Kierkegaard*, Oxford, 1938, p. 12.

work on Kierkegaard's philosophy of religion by declaring that
' no student of Kierkegaard who is sympathetic to his great
inward struggle to arrive at the Truth upon which he could live
and die, who has a measure of appreciation for his tremendous
dialectic powers and brilliant literary talents, could desire to
furnish an estimate of his philosophy, for he finds himself under
judgement.'[1] The fact is that there is no general agreement
amongst the scholars about the interpretation of the whole of
Kierkegaard's work. The literature dealing with it is vast indeed ;
yet, strangely enough, the core of his work remains something of
a mystery or an enigma. Herr Aage Henriksen says that there are
three main points of view which can be distinguished. They
' group themselves in two pairs of contrasts ; opposed to the
contention that the study of Søren Kierkegaard should aim at
understanding the expression, the literary form, stands the view
that the contents, the thoughts and ideas, are the central thing.
The group of enquirers who study the contents divide into two
formations, one of which maintains that the individual works
should be understood as parts of the totality of the production,
the other, that it is the history of Søren Kierkegaard's spiritual
development which unites the production.'[2] It seems to us that
whereas it is true to say that Kierkegaard's life was in a very real
sense the explanation of his work the second of these three points
of view is by far the most reasonable and the one which does
greatest justice to Kierkegaard's work. We do not wish to
be cavalier in our treatment of this point, but one can hardly
say that Kierkegaard is important only for the literary form
of his work. It may be true that a study of this form can give the
student of Kierkegaard valuable clues. Indeed Prof. Billeskov
Jansen of Copenhagen has argued that this is so in his *Det
Litterar Kunst af Søren Kierkegaard*. This is, however, a different
thing from saying that all he has to do really is to look at this
literary form. Then again, whilst we do not deny that many of
Kierkegaard's ideas developed out of particular situations in his
life we insist that there is in his work a certain unity which makes
the total output the continual development of a theme. In this

---

[1] Thomte, *Kierkegaard's Philosophy of Religion*, Oxford, 1949, p. 204.
[2] Henriksen, *Methods and Results of Kierkegaard Studies in Scandinavia*, Copenhagen,
p. 11.

way then we seek to resolve this difficulty about the interpretation of the whole of Kierkegaard's work.

We have mentioned the religious inspiration of Kierkegaard's work. It may be questioned whether this religious character which, all agree, is so prominent a feature of his work is not also a disadvantage as well as an advantage. Many would hesitate to describe Kierkegaard as a philosopher because of this.[1] Thus Guido de Ruggiero makes this enlightening, if also mistaken, comment : ' Kierkegaard is not a philosopher in the traditional sense of the word, but he is a religious soul, who, battling against philosophy, has philosophized in spite of himself.'[2] It seems to us very questionable whether Kierkegaard is a philosopher ' in spite of himself ', a ' médécin malgré lui '. It would be much truer to say that, though Kierkegaard's main concern was to point out the error of the Hegelian treatment of Christian faith he did this by using concepts of which he gave greater clarification than anyone else. Indeed he deliberately called for a new way of looking at philosophy and a new consideration of problems which had been neglected. Thus Herman Diem says that ' Kierkegaard did not think *now* as a theologian and *now* as a philosopher but thinks *always* as a Christian. So far as he investigates the possibilities of immanent thought with the means of natural thought it might be said that he thinks as a philosopher. But . . . it is a Christian philosophy.' For it is ' a philosophy after Christianity or after the man has become a Christian. And so the relationship for him is not that of philosophy to Christianity but that of Christianity to Christian knowledge or . . . if you will . . . to Christian philosophy.'[3] Yet this is to claim too much again. It is true that Kierkegaard never works on a strict principle of the division of labour so that one book is philosophical and the other theological. The point is, however, that in the context of theology he makes philosophical assertions as well as purely theological ones. In a real sense the question for him was that of the relation of philosophy to Christianity, and he sought to show that the claims of Christianity did not depend on philosophy. What

---

[1] Cp. Father Copleston's review of Thomte's book in *Philosophy*, January, 1950, p. 87.

[2] Guido de Ruggiero, *Existentialism*, Secker and Warburg, 1946, p. 24.

[3] H. Diem, *Philosophie und Christentum bei Soren Kierkegaard*, 1929, pp. 333, 345–7.

Diem does make clear, however, is that Kierkegaard's philosophy
is an integral part of his work.

Let us now try to trace the development in Kierkegaard's
thinking about faith. The actual influences that can be discerned
will be dealt with in another chapter, and for the moment our
concern is to show how Kierkegaard moved from what may be
called a philosophical view of Christianity to the position that
Christianity has nothing to do with philosophy. Our starting-
point is the summer of 1835. By this time he was a student in the
University of Copenhagen and was a leading figure in its social
life. His life was in fact somewhat bohemian, and in the summer
of 1835 his father gave him money for a tour of Seeland, in the
hope that he would return reformed. Lowrie points out that the
result of the tour was to deepen Søren Kierkegaard's romanticism.[1] After his return to Copenhagen Kierkegaard made some
comments in the *Journal* on Christianity. An entry of October
17th states that he had come to the conclusion that philosophy and
Christianity cannot be united.

> ' Philosophy and Christianity tolerate each other yet
> never unite (Cf. the scholastic saying : that something can be
> true in Philosophy which is false in Theology) . . . . I will
> suppose . . . a philosophy after Christianity . . . so Philosophy
> would . . . involve its total ruin.'[2]

The same view is expressed in a somewhat later entry which says
that he has ' tried to show why Christianity and Philosophy
cannot be reconciled '. He finds that there is a ' curiously oppres-
sive air ' in Christianity and speaks of ' the Christians ' in a very
aloof fashion.[3] His position now was that of dissatisfaction with
the two possible ways of upholding Christianity's truth—orthodoxy and rationalism.

> ' I grew up, so to speak, in orthodoxy ; but as soon as I
> began to think for myself the tremendous colossus began to
> totter . . . . Rationalism . . . cuts rather a poor figure.'[4]

More than this we do not know of his views in 1835, but obviously
they were in no sense expressive of a religious faith. The following
year they were already undergoing change. Having rejected

---

[1] Lowrie, *Kierkegaard*, Oxford, 1938, pp. 106–7.   [2] *Papirer* I A 94.
[3] ibid. I A 99 (Journals 32).   [4] ibid. I A 72 (Journals 16).

Christianity for philosophy he now became less and less confident
of finding satisfaction there either. In the winter of 1835 he had
started reading the work of Johan Georg Hamann, the enigmatic
'Magus of the North'. This is doubtless what produced the
profound dissatisfaction with the Hegelian philosophy which he
felt increasingly in these years. Until this time the Hegelian
philosophy was more or less the only philosophy that Kierkegaard
knew. Strangely enough it was only a year later that Kierkegaard
read Hegel seriously. This does not mean that the Hegelian
philosophy was unknown to him. He must have been familiar
with Hegelianism because he had studied under J. L. Heiberg,
the leading exponent of Hegelianism in Denmark. However,
reading Hamann made him now move away from the position
which naturally enough he had taken from his teacher. The
reverent way in which he hails Hamann as 'Emperor' in the
first reference to him in the *Journal*[1] makes it clear that this was
indeed a revolution in the history of Kierkegaard's thought.
Lowrie tends to overemphasise the part Hamann played in this
stage of Kierkegaard's development,[2] and he does not give Poul
Martin Møller the credit he deserves. Kierkegaard himself gives
us reason to think that Møller had been one of the great influences
in his life. The original dedication of *The Concept of Dread*
described Møller as 'the mighty trumpet of (Kierkegaard's)
awakening'. It would appear that Kierkegaard abandoned the
path of perdition as a result of the warning that Møller gave him
—'You are so completely polemical that it is terrible'. Prof.
Frithiof Brandt has commented on this word 'polemical' thus :

> 'There are two levels in the meaning of the word, an
> upper intellectual layer, and a deeper existential one. To be
> polemical does not only mean *L'esprit de contradiction*, to
> protest intellectually, . . . the word has a darker meaning and
> implies a nihilistic point of view, a personal nihilism, if you
> will. A man who is completely polemical has a negative
> relation to, or is in opposition to, the established forms of
> life. That is how Kierkegaard always uses the word and that
> is how he understood Møller.'[3]

[1] *Papirer* I A 234.
[2] Vide Lowrie, *op. cit.*, pp. 164–5.
[3] Brandt, *Den unge Kierkegaard*, 1929, p. 344, cited by Dru, *Journals of Søren Kierke-gaard*, p. xxxii.

Amongst his teachers at the University there was none perhaps who influenced Kierkegaard so much as Møller. Høffding says : ' Poul Møller must particularly be remembered when we talk of Søren Kierkegaard's older contemporaries—he it was who stood closest to Kierkegaard in personal relations.'[1] Møller had once been much taken up with Hegel's philosophy but later he became its critic. He lectured on the History of Philosophy, but it is obvious from his *Obiter Dicta*, for instance, that he had a keen appreciation for the more personal aspects of philosophy. In the draft version of a lecture about feeling Møller expresses his demand for a personal understanding of the nature of truth. For this reason Høffding says that he has an interesting place in the history of Danish philosophy as Kierkegaard's forerunner. Møller, like his friend and colleague Sibbern, had been influenced by Schelling. It is possible that he awakened in Kierkegaard an interest in Schelling, but we cannot pursue this question further. It will be more useful for us now to show Kierkegaard's development under the direct influence of Hamann ; for the influence of Møller would certainly give greater weight to the enthusiasm that Kierkegaard already felt for Hamann. Perhaps the most significant piece of evidence is a quotation from Hamann which we find in the Journal for September 12th, 1836 :

> ' Is it not an old idea that you have often heard from me : *incredibile sed verum ?* Lies and novels must be plausible, also hypotheses and fables ; but not the truths and fundamental propositions of our faith.'[2]

Of equal significance is the fact that on September 10th, the date of the first reference to Hamann, Kierkegaard turned back to his entries of October 17th and 19th, 1835, in the *Journal* and writes a marginal note about Hamann. The entry refers to Hamann's comment on Hume's concluding paragraph in his chapter on Miracles in the *Inquiry*. Hamann remarks that Hume, though he may have been mocking, nevertheless was quite right in saying that Christian faith is always a miracle. In October and November 1836 Kierkegaard began to move clearly towards his new position. By this time he was so greatly influenced by Hamann that he describes himself as

[1] P. M. Møller, *Efterladte Skrifter*, III, Copenhagen 1856. Cp. Hoffding, *Søren Kierkegaard som Filosof*, Copenhagen, 1892, p. 24. [2] *Papirer* I A 237.

one asleep waiting to be wakened. We notice too that he criticises the Idealist philosophers in no uncertain terms. ' What Schleiermacher calls " Religion " and the Hegelians " Faith " is,' he says, ' nothing but the first immediate condition for everything—the vital fluidum—the spiritual atmosphere we breathe in—and which cannot therefore with justice be designated by those words.'[1] Fichte's idea of immortality, he says in November, is an empty thing. ' Fichte threw his empirical ballast overboard and turned turtle.'[2]

The year following his discovery of Hamann was a most important one in Kierkegaard's development. This year saw the growth of the thinker in him as a result of a profound study of the German philosophy of religion, and in particular, the work of the philosopher Hegel. It began with his reading of P. M. Møller's article on ' The Immortality of the Soul ', published in a Danish monthly journal in January 1837. The footnotes referred to J. H. Fichte's book, *The Idea of Personality and of Individual Continuation*. This and other works of Fichte Kierkegaard read and studied, during the early months of 1837. He also came across Fichte's Journal, the *Journal of Philosophy and Speculative Theology*, and in May he was reading the Hegelian Journal—*Zeitschrift für spekulative Theologie*. He was much impressed by the work of Daub and studied carefully the work of J. Eduard on faith and knowledge, *Vorlesungen über Glauben und Wissen*. There is an extract from Heiberg's lectures on logic in his papers and we also find that he was attending Martensen's lectures on dogmatics. At this time, then, Kierkegaard was seriously and carefully studying the position of Hegel and his School, reading the work not only of the disciples but of the master himself as well. However, this intensive study of Hegel but confirms Kierkegaard in his conviction that the starting-point must be inwardness. So he says in the *Journal* entry for July 9th, 1838 :

> ' I mean to labour to achieve a more inward relation to Christianity ; hitherto I have fought for its truth while in a sense standing outside it. In a purely outward sense I have carried Christ's cross, like Simon of Cyrene.'[3]

[1] *Journals*, 78 (I A 273). Cp. I A 328 (Dru 88).
[2] ibid., 84 I A 302.
[3] *Journals*, 211 (II A 232).

This is a hint of the doctrine of subjectivity which we shall see was the category Kierkegaard used to interpret Christianity. That he has now reached the opposite position to the one he expressed when he rejected Christianity in favour of philosophy we can see from this entry in the *Journal* of August 1st, 1838 :

> '*About the relationship between Christianity and philosophy.*'
> Motto :
>> ' If a body meet a body
>> Carrying a spade,
>> And if a body bears a rake,
>> Need either be afraid? '

This is far more important than the triviality of its expression would suggest. Dr. Lowrie rightly insists that it ' had immense significance for Søren Kierkegaard ',[1] which we can see from the fact that he repeated it almost without change on an undated loose sheet. The sixteen entries following this latter are comments on it. Perhaps the most important of them is this one :

> ' Motto (in Latin) : "Cursed be he who keeps swine and teaches his son Greek wisdom " Jewish edict of 60 B.C.
> ' Christianity will have no dealings with the philosophies, even if they are willing to divide with it the spoils ; it cannot endure that the King of Sodom should say, I have made Abraham rich.'

This makes it perfectly clear that what Kierkegaard now holds is that Christianity need not be the least bit afraid of philosophy because there is no connection between them. In fact, it is the difference between them which now occupies his mind. In 1839 he remarks that ' the paradox is above every system '[2] ; and in 1841 makes this cryptic entry ' the idea of philosophy is mediation—Christianity's is the paradox.'[3] This is Søren Kierkegaard the anti-Hegelian that we know so well. He perceived that the synthesis that Hegelianism offered really took too much for granted, and did not face up to the enormous qualitative difference between genuine faith and its speculative philosophy. The aim

---

[1] We quote this and Dr. Lowrie's translation of the poem from Lowrie, op. cit., p. 166. The entry is II A 239. The next entry we quote is II A 790.
[2] *Papirer* II A 439 (Dru 282).
[3] ibid., III A 108 (Dru 356).

of the Hegelian philosophy was a synthesis, and its method the mediation of opposites. Now, Christianity has no interest in the mediation of opposites. On the contrary, the distinguishing feature of Christianity is that it asserts the infinite difference between God and man whilst maintaining that Jesus is both God and man. Kierkegaard's philosophical position of 1834 which was essentially Hegelian has now gone completely and his work is henceforward a powerful polemic against Hegel.

The battle against Hegel began with *The Concept of Irony*, his Master's dissertation, published in 1841. (This discussion of irony ' with constant reference to Socrates ' is a most subtle and damaging attack (on Hegel). M. Pierre Mesnard remarks that the dissertation was doubly ironic in that, (*a*) though it purported to be a historical study, it was an attack on the System and (*b*) it was done in the Hegelian style.

> ' Le traducteur allemand du *Concept d'Ironie*, Wilhelm Rutmeyer, n'a donc pas tort déclarer que l'épreuve tourne mal pour Hegel (op. cit. p. 351), ni de dénoncer la perfidie cachée de cet innocent candidat. L'attitude de Kierkegaard dans toute cette affaire est manifestement ironique, ou pourrait même ajouter d'une ironie au second dégré. Le premier consistait à présenter sous l'estampille de l'université de Copenhague ses idées les plus sécrètes, cachées sous les espèces d'une étude historique (idem, ibidem, p. 343). Le second ne visait à rien moins qu'a fair aussi enrégistrer solennellement sa volonté déclarée de renverser le système et de trembler l'ordre établi et de se faire néanmoins recevoir toutes boules blanches par les réprésentants de la philosophie hégelienne et de la société bourgeoise.'[1]

It is somewhat disappointing to see M. Jean Wahl unable to grasp this when he expresses surprise at the Hegelianism of *The Concept of Irony*.[2] though he could see quite well that the total effect of the book was a refutation of the Hegelian System.[3]

At this time Kierkegaard broke his engagement with Regina Olsen—an event of the greatest importance and one which had a

---

[1] Pierre Mesnard, *Le vrai visage de Kierkegaard*, Beauchesne, Paris, 1948, pp. 278–9.
[2] Wahl, *Études Kierkegaardiennes*, Vrin, Paris, 1949, p. 94.
[3] ibid., p. 110.

decisive influence on him. There can be no doubt that from this
bitter experience more than one idea sprang. Yet it concerns
us here only in so far as it was what led him to flee to Berlin,
where in some six months he finished writing *Either-Or*.[1] Some
scholars would say that this book has no relevance at all
to Kierkegaard's Philosophy of Religion because it belongs to
the ' aesthetic ' stage in his authorship. Some such view has
apparently dominated Scandinavian research on Kierkegaard.[2]
According to it the individual works must be interpreted
separately and their peculiarities explained psychologically. This
is defended either on the ground that it is unwise to accept
Kierkegaard's retrospective interpretations, or by emphasising the
obvious changes he made in his thinking. Such reasons have led
many scholars, including Bishop Torsten Bohlin, to join in the
psychological study of Kierkegaard. But surely this is the least
interesting and profitable way to study Kierkegaard; for not only
does this kind of treatment give his work a merely historical
interest but it actually neglects the undeniable consistency which
is to be found in his writings. His works are indeed connected
with his private history and can be taken as expressions of his
spiritual development. However, this is not to deny that there is
a unity in the whole production due to the fact that the whole of
his work is the development of certain themes, the most fundamental of which we would say is the Principle of Subjectivity.
Either-Or, like *The Concept of Irony*, is a subtle attack on the System
whilst appearing to be an expression of Hegelianism. Like Hegel
Kierkegaard seems to emphasise the prime importance of ethics,
and yet even in his description of the ethical stage Kierkegaard
uses a religious category.[3] Indeed Kierkegaard's own comment
on *Either-Or* is most illuminating.

 ' My particular concern with the whole of *Either-Or* is :
 that it should be quite clear that the metaphysical significance at the bottom of the whole work leads everything
 back to the dilemma. The same thing is also at the bottom
 of the little philosophical essay : Tautology as the highest

---

[1] Kierkegaard broke off his engagement on October 11th and on October 25th,
1841, he sailed for Berlin. Vide Henriette Lund, *Memoirs*, p. 557. He returned to
Copenhagen on March 6th, 1842. The whole of *Either-Or* was written in Berlin.
[2] Vide Henriksen, op. cit., p. 12.
[3] *Either-Or*, vol. II.

principle of thought ;[1] that is to say (how many will understand it) if the principle of contradiction is true (and that is
expressed in ' either-or '), it is the scientific expression for
mediation, and is the only unity in which it can be resolved,
the only way in which the system is possible. It would
not be aesthetically correct to write a treatise on the principle
of contradiction in this work and so it is expressed personally
—but the same thing seen from a speculative point of view
(if one does not wish to ' go further ') is the apotheosis of
tautology——'[2]

It is difficult to understand the whole of this argument, and the
very brilliance of the language makes one feel that it could well
hide a certain looseness in the reasoning. Nevertheless, we
can construe it well enough for us to glean some valuable points.
Unless we misunderstand Kierkegaard completely he is saying
(a) that ' either-or ' indicates the principle of contradiction
which is presupposed in all thinking, (b) that if we wish to have
the unity which the systematic metaphysician has sought then we
must use ' mediation ', (c) that the rejection of this movement of
metaphysics means an apotheosis of tautology. This is a frontal
attack on the idea of embracing opposites which was the essence
of the Hegelian dialectic. The whole point of *Either-Or* was to
present the dilemma of opposites—either the aesthetical life or
the ethical life. It was not an attempt to merge them in a synthesis
but to preserve them clearly apart so that it could be seen that they
were the alternatives of a choice. The point is much clearer in
connection with the little essay on Tautology. Since we assume
that the Law of Contradiction is true we must maintain that the
only certain statement is a tautology. Now, it is perfectly clear
that the Law of Contradiction holds universally, is indeed the
presupposition of all thought. For instance, the Law of De
Morgan which is an attempt at proving both the Law of Excluded
Middle and the Law of Contradiction actually assumed the Law of
Contradiction. This is the statement of the Law :

$$\sim (p.\, q) \quad = \sim p.\, v \sim q \,(1)$$
$$\sim (p.\, v\, q) \quad = \sim p.\, \sim q \,(2)$$
$$p\, v\, q \quad = \sim (\sim p.\, \sim q) \,(3)$$

[1] ibid., vol. I, p. 30.   [2] *Journals* 405 ((III B 177).

But (3) only follows if we assume the principle $\sim (p. \sim p)$. The problem is then to see how we can ever move to the synthesis p^1 from the contradictories p and $\sim p$. And if this move is not made we can make only the following assertions

$$\sim p \, v \sim p \supset \, \sim p$$
$$p \, v \, p \supset p$$

These are the definitions of tautology. It might help us to grasp Kierkegaard's point better if we compared it with Hume's insight that no individual proposition about a contingent matter of fact can be established *a priori*. This means that if we wish to make a novel assertion then we assert something which is not true *a priori*, and conversely anything which is true *a priori* is not an empirical assertion and is therefore a tautology. It is, of course, also connected with Leibniz's distinction between truths of reason and truths of fact, which is one of the sources of empiricism. Kierkegaard's argument makes essentially the same criticism of *a priori* systematic thinking. His point is that the System does away with the dilemma that is the peculiar characteristic of contingency especially the contingent human situation. The System tells us nothing about man.

The struggle against Hegelianism now well and truly begun is continued in all Kierkegaard's work. *Fear and Trembling*, which was published in 1843, carries it a stage further by showing that in religion it is the individual which is all important. He does this by pointing to the fact that in his effort to obey the command of God Abraham places himself above the general ethical law. The sacrifice of Isaac illustrates a ' teleological suspension of the ethical '. In 1844 *Philosophical Fragments* was published, and here Kierkegaard deals explicitly with the nature of religious faith. The book takes as its theme the question whether eternal happiness can be founded on historical knowledge. Clearly we meet here Kierkegaard's opposition to the unhistorical way in which Hegel regarded Christianity and he reminds us of the important fact that in Christianity certain historical statements are given a non-historical significance which does not take away their historicity. The most important of these might be the statement that Jesus of Nazareth was the Christ. The real problem of the *Fragments* comes to light only when we consider its sequel *The*

Concluding Unscientific Postscript to the Fragments. This is even more explicitly concerned with the problem of Philosophy of Religion dealing as it does with the truth of Christianity. Kierkegaard begins by distinguishing the two ways in which we can raise the question of the truth of Christianity. These are the ' objective ' and the ' subjective ' ways.[1] He points out that what interests the speculative philosopher namely the ' objective ' question is of little importance to the existing religious man. What interests him most is the ' subjective ' question whether he himself believes or not. By maintaining the ' subjective ' emphasis Kierkegaard brings to the discussion a fresh emphasis which is valuable. This is indeed the value of any ' existentialist ' approach to the question of religion. In this respect the *fons et origo* of existentialism seems to us in fact to be more valuable than any of his successors, for he was able to preserve a delicate balance between what we may call autobiography and public description so as to give a comprehensive philosophical description of faith. This description thus yields a paradox—that faith is something strangely like subjective statements because it is essentially something about me, and yet it is never reducible to just this. When Kierkegaard says that faith is not interested in the proofs which the philosopher tries to find he does not mean to say that faith has nothing to do with thinking. What he had seen was that you cannot move from the System to faith without a leap. Yet Kierkegaard was not lacking in respect for philosophy, not even for the philosophy of Hegel.[2] A most unjust view of him, which is unfortunately very popular, is that which makes him a fanatical opponent of all rational or objective thinking and an equally fanatical advocate of a complete irrationalism.[3] Later we shall see both the foundation of fact that there is for this view and also the way in which it distorts the facts. Meantime we can see how erroneous it is from this very pregnant statement in the *Postscript*:

> ' It is easy enough to leap away from the toilsome task of developing and sharpening the understanding, and so get a louder hurrah, and to defend oneself against every accusa-

---

[1] *Concluding Unscientific Postscript*, pp. 23–4.
[2] Vide *Postscript*, pp. 106–8, 231, 275 ; *Journals* 495.
[3] Cp. R. Jolivet, *Introduction to Kierkegaard*, Muller, London, 1950, p. 95. E. L. Allen, *Kierkegaard His Life and Thought*, London, 1935, passim. The title of H. E. Weber's paper, ' *Zwei Propheten der Irrationalismus* ' suggests the same idea.

tion by remarking that it is a higher understanding. So the believing Christian not only possesses but uses his understanding, respects the universal-human, does not put it down to lack of understanding if somebody is not a Christian; but in relation to Christianity he believes against the understanding and in this case also uses the understanding—to make sure that he believes against the understanding. Nonsense he therefore cannot believe against the understanding, for precisely the understanding will discern that it is nonsense and will prevent him from believing it; but he makes so much use of the understanding that he becomes aware of the incomprehensible and then he holds to this, believing against the understanding.'[1]

Kierkegaard's rejection of philosophy's claim to decide the truth of faith poses a problem for us. We may say with Karl Barth that this is true or we may doubt it, as perhaps M. Jolivet does. Yet it is idle to say ' yes ' or ' no ' to this without seeing that it achieves a great deal in terms of our understanding what philosophy does for religion.

Kierkegaard laboured to show that the religious man was not dependent on any false or artificial security. If faith's certainty were a philosophical matter, that meant for Kierkegaard that there was something wrong with it. The point that he had grasped so surely was that faith begins when its certainty is inward. If it were a certainty that resulted from a metaphysical scheme then it could be held only as long as that metaphysics is held. Now this is patently not true of faith. The Church Fathers had very different metaphysical views but they were all certain of their faith. Moreover when philosophies were being displaced faith held its own. So Prof. H. A. Hodges rightly asks:

> ' Why should Christians fear in the presence of the crisis in philosophy? Only if they have reason to think that the crisis can touch their own faith; and this it can do only if their faith is somehow dependent on philosophy. Here then we reach the kernel of the question. So long as Christians retain the view characteristic of Thomism, but not confined to it, that Christian truth rests, at least in part,

[1] *Postscript*, p. 504.

upon foundations of metaphysical reasoning so long will
they be disturbed by every change of metaphysical fashion.'[1]

This is simply a restatement of the point Kierkegaard made so
clearly. And in making it he made some very illuminating
remarks about the problem which faith raises for philosophy.
This is the problem of saying that the religious position is something we know to be true when our polemic had been to distinguish faith from any metaphysical theory. Kierkegaard's
life-story is an illustration of the difficulty of this matter. When
he was prepared to abandon Christianity he had not learned that
faith was not created by philosophy and could not be destroyed
by it. In other words, he was not clear about the nature of his
own problem or the controversy between philosophy and
Christianity. Later when he had learned this he was still concerned to preserve faith's claim to know God. And it is just
here that the dilemma appears for the philosopher of religion.
Is he to say that faith is as objective as knowing that there are
external objects or is he to say that it is as subjective a thing as
knowing that I have a toothache?

This problem has become more pressing during recent years
as a result of the development of the linguistic way of doing
philosophy. Theologians and philosophers of religion have been
somewhat frightened by the way in which the linguistic philosophers have talked of the meaninglessness of metaphysics. For
instance the distinguished American philosopher, the late E. S.
Brightman says that the ' positivists ' argue that religious beliefs
are false because they are unverifiable, and he tries to combat
this view by saying that ' religious propositions may be verified,
although with less certainty than scientific ones '. The verification he has in mind is ' membership in a coherent experience
system '.[2] This is really to have the idea that the religious position
is like a scientific hypothesis. Now if Prof. Brightman had
looked more carefully at what the analysts were doing he would
have seen that this was a quite unsatisfactory way of putting
forward the claim of religion to be true. Dr. Mascall is similarly
too anxious to discredit the ' logical positivists' ' dissolution of

[1] H. A. Hodges, ' The Crisis in Philosophy,' *Reformation Old and New* (edited by
F. A. Camfield), London, 1947, p. 194.
[2] E. S. Brightman, *A Philosophy of Religion*, Skeffington, London, 1948, p. 266.

C

metaphysics by attacking the slogan ' the meaning is the method
of verification.'¹ This slogan had its value, but it was a slogan
and not a dogma. In the same way it is not making philosophy
trivial to say that it is an attempt to dissolve puzzles produced by
linguistic confusion. If it can be shown that the application of the
linguistic technique to theological problems yields results which
are not the least frightening, then it seems to us modern philosophy
of religion will regain its status and its self-confidence. It is to this
situation that perhaps Kierkegaard can best speak. For if his
work is examined in the light of what the linguistic philosophers
have taught us we will be the better able to see the puzzle of
religion and perhaps go some way towards solving it. The fact
that Kierkegaard was able to describe so carefully the situation
of the man who moves from unfaith to faith is the most important
point in favour of making him our guide. For as Wittgenstein
said ' the difficulty in philosophy is to remember ' and ' philosophy
is description '.

One last point, it is the Christian religion and Christian
faith that here concern us. For Kierkegaard this is the task
that was entrusted to him—to make clear to his age what Christianity was. And the distinguishing feature of this is the conviction,
as M. Gilson says, that ' One has spoken who is more than
prophet '. This will be where we shall move in the sphere of
Paradox. Gilson refers to Rudolf Otto and hails him as a theologian who has presented the problem of revelation in the proper
way. In his renowned *Idea of the Holy* Otto describes pains-
takingly what he calls ' the inner witness of the Holy Spirit ',
and in the last page he warns us that above that witness is the
Prophet, and that above the Prophet, there is such an One who
is more than a prophet. The very last words of his book tell us
who he is : ' He is the Son '.² It is here the real problem begins
according to Gilson. And it is quite true that only here do we
meet the specific problem of Christianity.

' Knowing as we do, that He who is more than Prophet
has spoken, what are we to do with His message? . . . That,
at last, is a Revelation worthy of the name ; not our own
revelation of God to ourselves, but the revelation of God

---

¹ Vide E. L. Mascall, *He Who Is*, Longmans Green, London, 1943, pp. 65–7.
² Rudolf Otto, *The Idea of the Holy*, London, 1923, p. 182.

Himself to us ... If we learn from the medieval theologians
what is faith in an objective truth, and what is an objective
philosophical knowledge, we shall find ourselves possessed
of both a Revelation and a Reason. There then will be something to harmonize, and anyone attempting to do it will end
at last in meeting the real problem.'[1]

This is altogether admirable; for it elucidates how extremely
complex a problem the philosophy of religion poses when it
asks for a logical description of Christian faith. There are two
issues involved. The one is the question of the nature of faith,
the epistemological problem. In what sense or how far is faith
knowledge? M. Gilson is quite right in indicating that we need
to know what objective knowledge is. But it will be sufficient
for our purpose if we can show that the religious man's assertion
' There is a God ' is not reducible to statements about his feelings
and is a statement for which in fact there are reasons. The other
issue is the way in which the Christian man makes historical
assertions that have religious significance. The advent of Jesus
the Christ is at once a historical and non-historical assertion. To
see these puzzles clearly we turn to Kierkegaard's themes of
subjectivity and paradox.

[1] E. Gilson, *Reason and Revelation in the Middle Ages*, London, 1939, pp. 98–9.

CHAPTER II

THE HISTORICAL SITUATION

We cannot have a proper estimate of Kierkegaard's contribution unless we know exactly what he was combatting. We have spoken of his work as an anti-helegian polemic and as the most powerful of all criticisms of Hegel's Philosophy of Religion. This will be disputed by two kinds of scholars. The first kind will insist that Kierkegaard was greatly influenced by Hegel and that his very polemic against Hegel is hegelian. We shall see later that this cannot be substantiated because the roots of Kierkegaard's thought are to be found in the work of those who opposed Hegel. His work is thus a continuation of this opposition. The other kind of scholar will argue that Kierkegaard's criticism of Hegel is not really of any great importance because Kierkegaard never really understood Hegel. He will also say perhaps that Hegel was in fact a precursor of Kierkegaard. This contention is supported by the theory that both Hegel and Kierkegaard were profoundly influenced by Hamann's romantic irrationalism. So it is said that Hegel was really part of the Romantic movement and not a philosopher of the Enlightenment. This is one of those historical paradoxes that are not as surprising as they appear to be. If we patiently unravel it and see it for what it is we shall be able to concede the truth of the statement whilst also seeing that it is not altogether true. The theory of the common source of Hegel's thought and Kierkegaard's is not something that we can adequately discuss here ; but its weakness will become obvious when we see that Hamann's influence on Kierkegaard was not decisive and that Hegel can be called a Romantic only with reservation.[1] What we shall try to do here is to give an account of the development of Hegel's thought showing how the System grew out of the early theological writings. It is true that we do not often think of these early works when we talk of Hegel as the metaphysician par excellence or the theologian of rationalism. Yet the very fact that a great rationalistic system grew out of these early writings is some ground for doubting

[1] It is also worth noting that Kierkegaard had little sympathy with Romanticism. Indeed philosophically he was opposed to both Romanticism and the Enlightenment.

whether they can change our usual way of looking at Hegel. However, we must see (a) in what sense it is quite true to say that Hegel is the forerunner of Kierkegaard and (b) in what sense it is equally true and more important to say that Kierkegaard's criticism of Hegel was perfectly just in so far as he understood clearly and described correctly the position he criticised.

Hegel was born in the year 1770, and thus grew up in the time when the Enlightenment was everywhere under attack. Poets and religious men were repelled by its dry rationalism and antipathy to the feelings and the passions ; political thinkers and enthusiasts found it could not compare with the inspiration the incipient nationalism gave them ; philosophers too were dissatisfied with it because the insistence on ideas being clear and distinct and on the limits of human knowledge hindered their desire to speculate. The Age of Reason was in decline and the Age of Emotion and Imagination was beginning to dawn. Romanticism has been described as an anti-scientific and anti-intellectualistic movement. In the seventeenth and early eighteenth centuries, when science was advancing rapidly there appeared to be no limit to the possible triumphs of the human intellect. There was no field in which this dispassionate analysis could not bring profit. The eighteenth century regarded it as its special task to apply this type of reasoning to ' moral subjects '. In the seminary at Tübingen, which Hegel entered in 1788, as in the Stuttgart Gymnasium, the atmosphere was still that of the Enlightenment. Outside the seminary and the Gymnasium, however, the impact of the new spirit was felt. It is clear that in the early years of his development Hegel was as much influenced by this new spirit as he was by the academic training he had received. By reading books and pamphlets Hegel was made aware of the movement and he was directly influenced by it. It would be a mistake, however, to romanticise the early Hegel after the fashion of Dilthey. It was Dilthey's interest in the romantics (Novalis and Schleiermacher, in particular) that led him to the study of the early Hegel, and his picture of the latter was coloured by his interest.

We shall now consider the essays which Herman Nohl collected under the title *Hegel's theologische Jugendschriften*. First, we have certain fragments which he wrote when he was about twenty-five years old. These give us a very clear picture of the way in which Hegel looked at Christianity and religion in general in this period. He makes a distinction between what he calls objective and subjective religion. Objective religion is what can be systematised, presented in a book or in a lecture ; subjective religion expresses itself in feelings and acts. Subjective religion is all that matters and is in fact pretty much the same in all good human beings, whatever their objective religion may be. In support of this Hegel quotes Lessing's *Nathan*, the moral of which was that we do not know which religion is true, and so should respect other religions and above all be moral. He differs from Kant in thinking that what is needed to make men moral is something in man's passionate nature. It is not the understanding that changes principles to practice, but rather love. Moral teachings must be authorised by reason, but they must also correspond with the level of morality that people have attained. Neither Reason nor Christianity will raise the masses to the level of the ethics of pure duty. Hegel is very scathing in his remarks about Christianity. He contrasts the religion of classical Greece with the official religion of his day. The contrast is presented in an extremely sarcastic way, and not even Jesus Christ escapes the lash of the young moralist. He reproaches the Reformers for their Christian police institutions and their subjection of Christianity to worldly powers. He charges Protestantism with the substitution of theological superstitions about original depravity for the real knowledge of the human soul. Christianity can do nothing for the masses and Christian institutions are abhorrent to him. Together with this hatred of Christianity goes a whole-hearted faith in *religion*. By religion he means a folk-religion, and this idea he had from Herder. The idealised picture of Greece was common to all the Romantics ; but in this varied influence we can discern that shade of colouring which takes us back to the Aufklärung. Hegel insists on the primacy of morals and the sovereignty of reason. Religion, he thought, should be the most important force for attaining morality which was the chief end of man. It should not be a theological affair but should appeal to the emotions and the imagination. The religion of Greece had done just this with its exquisite sense of beauty. So understood, religion would be the affair of the whole nation and not that of a special church. The doctrines of religion must not contain anything that universal human reason does not recognise. Such is the first period of Hegel's development, one in which Hegel appears as the almost-Romantic.

To understand the second period of Hegel's development we must understand the very puzzling relation between him and Kant. We are no longer talking of Hegel as a straightforward development from Kant. We bundle Kant into the basket of 'Empiricism' and Hegel into that of 'Idealism'. Thus we would perhaps hesitate were we asked whether Kant was a decisive influence on Hegel. However, there can be no doubt that Kant did influence Hegel very much in the seventeen-nineties. This influence is clearly discernible in the *Life of Jesus* which Hegel wrote in 1795. The previous contrast between the folk religion of Greece and Christianity now gives way to the contrast between the moral faith and the 'positive' (i.e. institutional) faith. In the essay Jesus appears to be nothing more than a teacher of Kantian ethics. The opening words are a definition of deity as pure reason without limitation. The story opens with his birth as the son of Mary and Joseph and ends with his burial. Jesus preaches the doctrine of universal ethics—'What you can will to be a universal law among men, valid also against yourselves, according to that maxim act—this is the basic law of ethics, the content of all the sacred books of all people.' Hegel's Jesus regards reason and morality as the ultimate authorities and his God is pure reason who can be moved only by the eternal moral law. This thorough demythologising of the Gospel story of Jesus was the way in which Hegel tried to express the Kantian idea of religion and morals as pure reason. The moral demands gain force from this human figure.

The question which Hegel was now forced to ask was this : If the religion of Jesus was this rational respect for the eternal moral law how did it come about that Christianity is a positive religion? This is the question he tries to answer in *The Positivity of the Christian Religion* (1795). Once again he tells us that his basic assumption is that the end and essence of all true religion is the morality of man. He defines positive as meaning founded on authority and placing the worth of man not at all, or at least not only, in morality. 'A positive religion is contrasted with natural religion. . . . It is clear from this very contrast that a positive religion is a contranatural or a supernatural one, containing concepts and information transcending understanding and reason and requiring feelings and actions which would not come naturally to men.[1] The point of the essay is to show that the seeds of positivity are to be found in Jesus' own teaching and conduct despite the fact that there seems to be a chasm between the morality of pure reason, which the *Life of Jesus* had ascribed to him, and the positive thing Christianity had become. Jesus is not blamed for this : the Jews would not, thinks Hegel, respond to any other approach. However, the fact is that the woeful beginning of positivity or institutionalism lies in Jesus' unavoidable connection of his own person with the moral law man must venerate. Hegel is very sarcastic in his criticisms of Christianity.

> 'Every church gives out that its own faith is the *non plus ultra* of truth, it starts from this principle and assumes that its faith can be pocketed like money. The faith really is treated like this ; every church holds that nothing in the world is so easy to find as truth ; the only thing necessary is to memorize one of its catechisms. For the churches it is false to say[1] :

> > ' ''Tis earnestness that flinches from no toil
> > That alone can catch the gurgle of truth's deep-hid spring'
> 'The church offers truth in the open market ; the stream of ecclesiastical truth gurgles noisily in every street, and any wayfarer can drink his fill of it.'[2]

Hegel rejects too the traditional account of the expansion of Christianity. The success of the Christian religion, he believes, was not at all because it gave enlightenment or fresh insights— 'in the expansion of Christianity use was made of everything and anything rather than reason and intellect'. The real reason was the spirit of the age, a spirit of slavery which found its counterpart and expression in the doctrines of an objective God and a currupt human nature. Hegel's estimate of Christianity is clearly overwhelmingly negative.

[1] Hegel, *Early Theological Writings* (trans. Knox and Kroner) 1948, p. 167.
[2] op. cit., p. 134.

This period marks the end of a definite stage in Hegel's development. The tone of *The Spirit of Christianity and Its Fate* (1798–9) is different from that of *The Positivity of The Christian Religion*. This might lead us to imagine that Hegel was moving from his anti-Christian position to a more sympathetic estimate of Christianity and that he was now something of a Christian mystic. This seems very doubtful. The essay shows in fact nothing more than the synthesis between Hellenism and Kantianism which Hegel had been able to effect by turning back to German classicism. While the Romantics pined with longing for ancient Greece Hegel found in Goethe a present embodiment of what he had admired in Greece. For the Greeks the highest thing was beauty and this idea is the nerve of Greek religion. For Kant, on the other hand, the primary thing was morality and this is the substance of his religion. These are the two influences that we have seen in Hegel's earlier writing. What he has now achieved is the union of these two different ideas. If religion is to be concerned with beauty, and morality yet be the chief end of man, then the highest thing is moral beauty. This means a break with both the Romantic cult of Beauty and the Kantian idea of Duty. We can see how Hegel has abandoned Kantianism if we consider what he has to say about Jesus in this essay.

> ' One who wished to restore man's humanity in its en-
> tirety could not possibly have taken a course . . . which
> simply tacks on to man's distraction of mind an obdurate
> conceit. To act in the spirit of laws could not have meant for
> him " to act out of respect for Duty and to contradict inclina-
> tions ", for both " parts of the spirit " (no other words can
> describe this distraction of soul) just by being thus diver-
> gent would have been not in the spirit of the laws but against
> that spirit, one part because it was something exclusive and
> so self-restricted, the other because it was something sup-
> pressed.
> ' This spirit of Jesus, a spirit raised above morality, is
> visible, directly attacking laws, in the Sermon on the Mount,
> which is an attempt, elaborated in numerous examples, to
> strip the laws of legality, of their legal form. The Sermon
> does not teach reverence for the laws ; on the contrary, it

exhibits that which fulfils the law but annuls it as law and
so is something higher than obedience to law and makes law
superfluous.'[1]

This shows quite clearly that Hegel was deliberately rejecting
Kant's idea that morality which was obedience to an absolute law
was the heart of religion. The result of such an idea, he thinks,
is the division of man against himself. It was precisely such a
division that Judaism had effected, reducing man to the two elements of conscience, the master, and the man himself, the slave.
This division Jesus healed, restoring man's essential unity. This
was his great contribution. Against the commands which presuppose something resisting the commander he set virtue as a
loving disposition and this is congruent with both law and inclina-
tion. This idea of a virtue beyond morality is surprisingly like
Nietzsche however much it resembles the Pauline idea of the Christ
as the end of the law and its πληρωμα. Certainly we cannot identify
it with the latter.

Again, if we examine what Hegel means by faith we shall see
that here too we must hesitate to say that he had moved to a
Christian position.

> 'Faith in Jesus means more than knowing his real
> personality, feeling one's reality as inferior to his, in might
> and strength, and being his servant. Faith is a knowledge of
> spirit through spirit, and only like spirits can know and
> understand one another; unlike ones can know only that
> they are not what the other is. Differences in might and
> spirit, in degree of force, is not unlikeness, but the weaker
> hangs on the superior like a child, or can be drawn up to
> him. So long as he loves beauty in *another* and so long as
> beauty is in him though undeveloped . . . so long is he still
> at the level of faith alone. As Jesus says (John xII, 36):
> Until you have light yourselves, believe in the light and
> thereby become yourselves children of the light.'[2]

Later in the same work Hegel discusses knowledge of the relation
of Jesus to God in terms of this notion of spirit knowing spirit.[3]

[1] op. cit., p. 212.
[2] op. cit., pp. 239–40. The text has been wrongly translated. Westcott goes so
far as to say that the temporal sense of ὡς slides into the regulative i.e. 'since'.
It is noteworthy that the Vulgate renders the clause ' Dum lucem habetis '.
[3] op. cit., pp. 266–9.

The essence of this relationship can be grasped only by faith, and so Jesus had demanded faith in himself. Hegel distinguishes this kind of faith from any other kind of faith by saying that it is characterized by its object (Gegenstand) the divine. Faith in a mundane reality is acquaintance with an object (Objekt). Since God is spirit and so can only be known by spirit he cannot be an object (Objekt) as distinct from a subject : he is the object (Gegenstand) of faith—he in whom we believe. Conversely because faith in God is possible we know that we are spirits. We know that there is in the believer himself ' a divine element which rediscovers itself, its own nature, in that on which it believes '. ' Hence faith in the divine grows out of the divinity of the believer's own nature ; only a modification of the Godhead can know the Godhead.'[1] There is a clear distinction drawn between those who have faith in the light and those who are sons of the light. ' Between those who only have faith in the light and those who are the children of light there is a difference similar to that between John the Baptist, who only bore witness of the light, and Jesus, the light individualised in a man. . . . All thought of a difference in essence between Jesus and those in whom faith in him has become life, in whom the divine is present, must be eliminated.'[2]

In 1800 Hegel wrote the *Fragment of a System* in which he summed up his views as they had taken shape up to that time. It is very difficult to know what to make of this fragment if only because we have but two of the forty-seven sheets which originally composed Hegel's manuscript. In both of these, however, he is apparently concerned with the same problem as he had dealt with in *The Spirit of Christianity*, the problem of unifying opposites. He takes up the idea of life again and reinterprets it so as to make it yield the solution of his problem. Life ' is the union of union and nonunion. . . . Within the living whole there are posited at once death, opposition and understanding, because there is posited a manifold that is alive itself and that, as alive, can posit itself as a whole '.[3] Consequently this living whole is something partial and this partial character of the living being is only transcended in religion. Understanding must be reconciled with life—this was what Hegel proposed to himself as his life-task.

[1] ibid., p. 266.   [2] op . cit., p. 268.   [3] ibid., p. 312.

But as yet he could not see that anything except religion did this. The action of philosophical thought was quite the opposite—it is the murder of the unity with which life presents us. The essential task of the philosopher is that of distinguishing opposites, and this very action destroys life. This is very much like Wordworth's

> ' Sweet is the lore which Nature brings ;
> Our meddling intellect
> Mis-shapes the beauteous forms of things :—
> We murder to dissect.'

Hegel recognises that there is ' one kind of opposition to be found in the multiplicity of living beings. . . . The multiplicity of life has to be thought of as divided against itself '.[1] The division is rather peculiar. One part of the multiplicity is to be regarded as solely in opposition and the other purely something related. The unity is called an organization or individual. Now, this idea of individuality includes opposition to infinite variety *and* a relation to it. It is difficult to understand what Hegel is saying here. His real point seems to be that the individual exists only in a totality, and that our notion of the individual is derived from that of the totality. This is clearly the germ of something which we can recognise as distinctly Hegelian—the idea that the individual's existence is dependent on the whole of which it is a part. But it is only the germ because the surprising thing about the *Fragment* is that it lays down definite limits to philosophy.

> ' Philosophy therefore has to stop short of religion because it is a process of thinking and, as such a process, implies an opposition with nonthinking processes as well as the opposition between the thinking mind and the object of thought. Philosophy has to disclose the finiteness in all finite things and require their integration by means of reason. In particular, it has to recognize the illusions generated by its own infinite and thus to place the true infinite outside its confines.'[2]

Since he would appear to have such a high estimate of religion Hegel's understanding of worship is very important. However,

---

[1] op.. cit., p. 309.　　　　　　　　　　[2] op. cit., p. 313.

this is discussed on Sheet 47 which begins in the middle of a sentence so that it is almost impossible to conjecture what the whole argument was. Nor is it too clear how we are to interpret the fragment that we have. Prof. Richard Kroner interprets it in an explanatory footnote as presenting the contrast between the worship of God as an object and the worship of him as an infinite life in which the worshipper shares Religion in its highest form, conceives of God not as a mere object separate from man but as an infinite life united with men. The act of worship then becomes the union of subject and object.

During the spring and summer of 1801 Hegel wrote his first important book, *The Difference between the Systems of Fichte and Schelling*. In this book Hegel assumes the role of an umpire between the opponents, reviewing the work of both men with equal sympathy and with a critical independent judgment. He tries to show that when the two systems have been shorn of their errors they can supplement each other. Fichte had recognized that the Absolute has to be conceived as absolute Ego, not as absolute object; and this Hegel decided to maintain. On the other hand Schelling was nearer the truth than Fichte when he posited the principle that would unite subjectivity and objectivity. This unification of subjectivity and objectivity is the desideratum; but a unification that is brought about by the denial of the opposition is useless. If the absolute identity is alive the opposites must be contained in it. The problem had presented itself for Hegel previously as one of reconciling intuition and reflection. He returns to this and says that intuition itself has to become reflective. The intellect must transcend itself in a rational fashion, shattering its own destructive separations, and so achieve by self-development what had before been done by a *deus ex machina*. 'Speculation demands in highest synthesis . . . even the annihilation of the reflective consciousness itself. . . . This right of mere reflection and calculating understanding is the noon of Life, and in it both life and reflection can meet.'[1] In other words those very contradictions that analysis lays bare are what will push us on to speculation. This becomes clear from this later remark : ' If one reflects merely on the formal element in speculation and clings to the synthesis of knowledge in a purely

[1] *Werke*, I p. 188.

analytic form, then the antimony, the self-cancelling contradiction, is the highest formal expression of knowledge and of truth.'[1] What we have here is the transition from the uncertainty of the *Fragment* to the later Hegel of the *Phenomenology*.

The winter of the following year was also an important time for Hegel and during this period he wrote a manuscript which was published posthumously. The first editors, Ehrenberg and Link, gave it the title *Hegel's First System*. It is only a fragment but it shows us the plan which Hegel had for his speculative construction. In effect, what he does is to try and produce the composite form of knowledge which in the pamphlet on Fichte and Schelling he had declared necessary. Logic is the systematic conquest of the contradictions metaphysics produces. Therefore Logic is the science of the basic principles of existence as well as thought. The problem for Hegel now was to preserve the unity which he had discovered in life when he brought this within a philosophical system. In a way this was the same problem as Kant had faced in the *Critique of Pure Reason*—that is, the problem of the limits of knowledge. Kant's solution was taken up by Fichte, and for Hegel the task of philosophy now was to follow out the path which Kant had opened up and take the last step. This last step will be the production of a science that will at once show the limits of knowledge and transcend it. This is what Hegel calls ' Logic '. Logic shows how thought must be transcended because it leads to contradictions. This Logic is, of course, very different from the traditional idea of logic—this is a dynamic thing. The new Logic, because it is the science of living truth, must be a living thing. The old logic would dissect thought and so present us with the *disjecta membra*—propositions and so on—which are not thought itself at all. Thought is the self-actualisation of the living self. How then are we to make logic contain the living active self? Hegel's answer is that his logic can do this because it is a logic of life. This means four things for him :

1. It is a logic of spirit.
2. It is a logic of reason.
3. It is a logic of intuition.
4. It is a logic of Being and Reality.

[1] *Werke*, I pp. 192–3.

It is a logic of spirit because spirit reunites what the intellect has separated. It is a logic of reason for reason is speculative. Intuition underlies the self as thinking and the self as thought, and is both opposed to and at one with understanding. Finally, it is a logic of being so that the objects of thought move within it. The objects of the logic are concepts which are not mere subjective ideas but rather form and content at the same time. It is clear then that this Logic is dialectical and moves, like thinking, from opposites to opposites in the pattern of thesis, antithesis and synthesis.

In his concept of *Geist* Hegel found the inseparable connection between the human and the divine. *The Spirit of Christianity* tells the story of this his greatest discovery. His idea of mind unites Fichte's Absolute Ego with Schelling's Absolute as the Identity of objectivity and subjectivity, of Ego and Nature. The origin of this new metaphysic is to be seen in the draft of 1801 where we see logic being merged into metaphysics. In 1801 Hegel also wrote an essay on the relation between faith and knowledge which was published in *The Critical Journal of Philosophy*. This problem had always been a pressing one for Hegel. The ultimate decisions in philosophy, he thought, depend upon the answer to the question of how far the truths of faith can be grasped by the intellect. ' The contrast between faith and reason is in our time a contrast within philosophy itself.'[1] It appears in fact as the question of knowledge of things-in-themselves. Do we know things as they really are? If we do then we know them as God knows them. Now Kant had seen the connection between epistemology and the knowledge of God and he had denied any knowledge of things-in-themselves. Hegel regards this as the outgrowth of Protestantism which had broken the scholastic union of faith and knowledge by the distinction between reason and revelation. This is not without its dangers. ' The beautiful subjectivity of Protestantism is transformed by the Enlightenment into an empirical subjectivity, and the poetry of its grief . . . into the prose of a satisfaction with this finite world.'[2] Nor had Kant and Fichte satisfactorily remedied this basic defect. ' Man and mankind are their absolute principles, namely, a fixed and insurmountable finitude of reason, rather than a reflected splendour of eternal

[1] *Werke* I, 3.   [2] ibid., p. 10.

beauty.'[1] In fact, the only remedy that is satisfactory, according to Hegel, is the creation of a new religion by philosophy. Philosophy is called upon to do what faith alone can never do—to reconcile completely the absolutely opposite. The problem of the relation of faith to speculation had now been solved for Hegel, and this was the position he continued to hold.

One of Hegel's purposes in writing the *Phenomenology of Mind* was the reconciliation of the individual and mankind. This is done by saying that the universal mind is operative in every individual mind and is the very substance of it. History as an empirical science only narrates what happened and how those events are connected according to the principle of causality and does not disclose the inner coherence of those events which is determined by the ultimate purpose of the mind. The study of this coherence can only be said to be empirical inasmuch as it presupposes a knowledge of the facts ; and it is essentially a speculative study. Hegel uses historical figures and events to show the principal steps in the development of mind's self-knowledge. In this connection Hegel reinterprets the idea of the ' presents ' as the union of the *hic et nunc* and the eternal present. The task he undertook was that of showing the inner unity of past and present. There is really present only so much of the past as was eternal in the past and capable of going on living.

> ' The goal, which is Absolute knowledge of Spirit knowing itself as Spirit, finds its pathway in the recollection of spiritual forms as they are in themselves and as they accomplish the organization of their spiritual kingdom. Their conservatism, looked at from the side of their free phenomenal existence in the sphere of contingency is *History* ; looked at from the side of their conceptually comprehended organization, it is the *Science* of phenomenal knowledge.'[2]

Hegel is concerned not with events but with their meaning and their contribution to the solution of the problem called ' Man '. The *Phenomenology* is the history of man as the image of God.

This leads us to Hegel's discussion of Being. Being and Knowledge are but two sides of the same penny. They are distinguishable, nevertheless ; and Being is the more fundamental

[1] ibid., p. 15.
[2] Hegel, *Phenomenology of Mind* (trans. Baillie, London 1931), p. 808.

category, since it is the presupposition of all logical judgments
and of all knowledge. Being is all-embracing, but it is itself
embraced in thought. It is impossible to separate one aspect, for
Being comprises all the differences of content and form, of quality
and quantity, of finitude and infinity, etc. But it is itself more
general than any of these particular determinations of Being.
Being is Being, but it is also a concept, and it is as a concept that
it figures in the Logic. On the other hand, the Logic, just because
it is a logic of Being, is not only a logic but also an ontology and
a metaphysic. And the concept is therefore not only a concept
but Being, Life, Reality itself. The category of Being, however,
simply because it is the beginning, can only be preserved by
moving on into transformation. In so far as Being is all-inclusive
its contrary is absolute Nothing. It is by passing into this and
opposing it that Being is preserved. This is the mysterious
dialectic which is ' the secret of Hegel '.

We shall now consider how Hegel interprets specifically
Christian themes. We shall see first how he regards the relation
of God to the World, and then the way he interprets the Incarnation, and finally what status he gives to religious faith. First,
God is not personal. For God is identical with Absolute Reality,
and Absolute Reality can only adequately be conceived as a society
of persons, which is a perfect unity but not a person. It is not
always made clear that for Hegel God was not a person, and this
misinterpretation is in part due to the fact that he so often uses
the word God instead of Absolute Reality. But the question now
arises, if God is Absolute Reality does he not therefore include
everything which exists? It is true that Hegel himself often
protests against this view. But if we consider what he says we
find that what he denies is that God is identifiable with the ' facts
of experience '. But it is still true that for him God is identical
with all that really exists. For these facts we have spoken of do
not really exist—they are but inadequate views of Reality. Therefore in so far as anything is real it is a part of God because God
is Absolute Reality.

' We have now reached the realised notion or conception
of religion, the perfect religion, in which it is the notion
itself that is its own object. We defined religion as being in
the stricter sense the self-consciousness of God. Self-

D

consciousness in its character of consciousness has an object, and it is conscious of itself in this object ; this object is also consciousness, but it is consciousness as object, and is consequently finite consciousness, a consciousness which is distinct from God, from the Absolute . . . . God . . . knows Himself in a consciousness which is potentially the consciousness of God, but is also this actually, since it knows its identity with God, an identity which is, however, mediated by the negation of finitude. . . . Finite consciousness knows God only to the extent to which God knows Himself in it.'[1]

Our next question is what meaning Hegel gave to the Incarnation. The first point is that it is the very nature of the Absolute Spirit to manifest itself in a number of individuals each of whom is a self-conscious person. But, besides this, Hegel says that the Spirit manifests itself in the form of finitude. This is ' an act of going out on the part of God into finitude, a manifesting of God in finitude, for finitude, taken in its proper meaning, implies simply the separation of that which is implicitly identical but which maintains itself in the act of separation.'[2] This view resembles the doctrine of Incarnation. But Hegel goes further and actually asserts the incarnation of very God in very man :

' In the Church Christ has been called the God-Man. This is the extraordinary combination which directly contradicts the Understanding ; but the unity of the divine and human natures has here been brought into human consciousness and has become a certainty for it, implying that the otherness or . . . the finitude . . . of human nature is not incompatible with this unity . . . . It involves the truth that the divine and human natures are not implicitly different.'[3]

However, this assertion is not as valuable, from a doctrinal standpoint, as on first glance it appears to be. For, according to Hegel, God is incarnate not in one man only but in all men and indeed in everything finite. The world of finitude is nothing other than God in one moment of the dialectical development of His nature. Thus it is not so much a matter of God being incarnate in finitude as finitude being an aspect of God. This leads

[1] Hegel, *Philosophy of Religion*, vol. II, p. 327.
[2] op. cit., III, 38.   [3] ibid., pp. 76–7.

us to ask what Hegel says about Jesus Christ. Obviously, Hegel would agree that he was God incarnate for the simple reason that he was a man. By the same token he is not the only incarnation of God. But Hegel discusses the special prominence of Jesus Christ in a little more detail than this. First, he says that it is necessary for the incarnation of God in a particular person to have special significance not because of anything in the nature of the incarnation of God but because men generally are unable to grasp the pure notion of incarnation.

> ' If Man is to get a consciousness of the unity of divine and human nature, and of this characteristic of Man as belonging to Man in general . . . then it must reach him in his character as Man in general . . .; it must come to him as representing Man in his immediate state, and it must be universal for immediate consciousness.
>
> The consciousness of the Absolute Idea which we have in thought, must therefore not be put forward as belonging to the standpoint of philosophical speculation . . . but must, on the contrary, appear in the form of certainty for man in general. . . . This Idea, namely the unity of divine and human nature, attains the stage of certainty that . . . it receives the form of immediate sense-perception. . . . This unity must accordingly show itself to consciousness in a purely temporal . . . in one particular man . . . who is at the same time known to be the Divine Idea.'[1]

Since, then, mankind in general cannot appreciate the truth of this Divine Idea a particular incarnation is necessary. But, on the other hand, because of its very particularity this can only be taken as an example of a truth which is absolutely universal.[2] The special significance of Jesus, then, is that he bears witness to a metaphysical truth—the unity of God and man. Of course, he does not bear witness to this *as* a metaphysical truth but he witnesses to it as a ' certainty and sensuous view ', as the ' immediate presence and certainty of the Divine '. Again, in the strictest sense, he is not even a teacher of this Idea. The immediate certainty of this unity of God and man runs through his teaching, but it is not explicitly enunciated very often. It is significant that

[1] op. cit., III, 72.   [2] Cp. ibid., 75.

the words of Jesus which Hegel regards as most important are
those in which he expresses his unity with the Father.[1] It is not
surprising, therefore, that in Hegel there is little value given to
the history of Jesus. The sole religious value of history is that
it is the vehicle of such and such truths ; stripped of this it is
no more significant than any other piece of history.

Finally, let us consider what status Hegel gives to religious
faith. Faith is a form of knowledge—but it is knowledge only in
a peculiar form. The divine content appears as knowledge of
the Divine. But this content, though it appears for the immediate
consciousness, is yet one in all things. So in fact this is but a
mirror of the Idea :

> ' The Idea is represented figuratively, known and fore-
> shadowed in the seed which is the fruit ; the fruit in its final
> character dies away in the earth, and it is through this nega-
> tion that the plant first comes into being. A history, a pic-
> torial representation, a description, a phenomenon of this
> sort can be elevated by Spirit to the rank of something
> universal, and thus the history of the seed or of the sun
> becomes a symbol of the Idea, but *only* a symbol.'[2]

The implication is that what we have in religion is a pictorial
representation of the ultimate Reality, Spirit. This means that
for Hegel the distinction between faith and knowledge is very
much like that which Plato drew in the *Republic*. To use the
latter's analogy the religious man is the prisoner in the cave who
does indeed see the appearances of things, but the philosopher
knows things as they are, for he is outside the cave.

> ' Religion itself is this action, this activity of the thinking
> reason, and of the man who thinks rationally—who as
> individual posits himself as the Universal, and annulling
> himself as individual, finds his true self to be Universal.
> Philosophy is in like manner thinking reason, only that this
> action in which religion consists appears in philosophy in
> the form of thought, while religion, as, so to speak, reason
> thinking naively, stops short in the sphere of general idea
> or ordinary thought.'[3]

[1] Cp. ibid., pp. 84 and 86.   [2] ibid.,p. 114.   [3] op. cit., I. p. 194.

For Hegel then the religious man does not know what he is saying—only the philospher can tell him what the truths are which he expresses in symbols. Religious faith is thus a peculiar kind of knowledge, or more exactly it is the raw material of knowledge. If we are to understand what faith is we must get beyond it to philosophy. Then we shall see that faith is the first stage on man's road to Ultimate Reality. We must reach it if we seek that goal ; but the goal is beyond it.

This account of the development of Hegel's philosophy has perforce been very brief, but we hope that we have been able to summarise clearly and justly the early ' theological ' work as well as the later more familiar work. His development was itself dialectical. He started as a devotee of the Enlightenment, passed through the influence of Romantic Hellenism and Kantianism, and came at last to a synthesis of these very different influences. Where he had previously attacked Christianity he came later to uphold it. However, even in his defence of Christianity he was a true son of the Enlightenment ; for he maintained in the end as in the beginning that the most important pursuit, above art and religion alike, was philosophy. Philosophy is the Judge of all things. We have seen that the early theological writings do not contribute anything very different to our estimate of Hegel's influence on theology—apart from the early hostility to Christianity. The essential idea of religion as folk religion, the understanding of the destiny of man in terms of something like the Nietzschean Superman,—these are hardly to be reckoned as valuable contributions to the elucidation of Christian faith. The way in which the themes of faith and the Incarnation are treated are very much like the later work. The religious position in this later work was really the more influential, and we can now summarise it briefly thus. God is not a person, but a community of persons. All finite things are incarnations of God and only as such have they any real existence. The special significance of Jesus Christ in regard to incarnation was that he bore witness to the truth of the unity of God and man in a form that was convenient for popular apprehension. Faith is the uncritical use of symbols which contain ideas that the philosopher can show to be true. It is not its own justification but can only be justified by philosophy. Being and knowledge are one and the same thing and they cannot be distinguished.

The development of Hegelianism in theology took the familiar pattern of dividing the movement into a left and right wing. Marheineke[1] came to be regarded as the leader of the Hegelian Right, and presumably Strauss or Feuerbach would represent the leader of the Left. At first a disciple of Schelling's, Marheineke found a new master in Hegel, and like Hegel he sought to raise faith to the higher plane of speculative understanding. His aim was to explain all the orthodox doctrines of the Church in an orthodox way in terms of the Hegelian philosophy. His developed views on dogmatics are given in the third edition of his *Die Grundlehre der Christlichen Dogmatik als Wissenschaft* (1847). When he published his first edition in 1819 he was still a disciple of Schelling's. The second edition which appeared in 1877 marks the change of view, and it is in this edition that Kierkegaard read the work.[2] The work of Daub and Marheineke illustrates the difficulties which faced Hegelians in their attempt to make faith metaphysics. Even after they had proved the metaphysical necessity of the union of the divine and human they could not relate this at all easily or naturally to the event of Jesus Christ. That Jesus Christ should be the point of this union is a pure accident. It is only with difficulty that Marheineke saves himself from adopting the same historical and moralistic position as the eighteenth century rationalists. For instance, the Ascension means for him ' the truth that religion which takes its origin from God, has no abiding place on earth, but necessarily returns whence it took its rise '. This uneasy alliance could not last very long and the Left wing represents the opposition to the alliance.

Of the Hegelian Left the most influential figure was Strauss.[3]

[1] Philip Konrad Marheineke (1780–1846) was born in Hanover on May 1st, 1780, and studied at Göttingen. He lectured at Erlangen and Heidelberg. In 1811 he was made *professor ordinarius* at Berlin where from 1820 onwards he was also a preacher at Trinity Church and worked with Schleiermacher.

[2] Vide *Papirer* I A 272. I C 25 is a reference to excerpts in Danish from the book. It is no. 644 in the catalogue and was bought in 1836.

[3] David Friedrich Strauss (1808–74) was born near Stuttgart on January 27th, 1808, and was educated at Tübingen. He heard Schleiermacher in Berlin in 1831, Hegel having died. He became acquainted with Hegel's disciples and during this year planned his great work on the Life of Jesus. He returned to Tübingen and after a short period of lecturing devoted his time to writing. He was appointed Professor of Theology in Zürich ; but as a result of the tremendous popular disapproval of the appointment he was pensioned off before he was installed.

His work centred upon the problem of the significance of the
historical Person of Jesus for the believer or for the Christian
Church. His famous *Life of Jesus* was published in 1835 and was
translated into English by George Eliot. It was a book of momen-
tous significance, because it showed that it could not be assumed
that Hegelianism and Christianity were but two different expressions of the same thing. The point of Strauss's *Life* is that the
Gospel narratives are a collection of myths which were formed
in the early Church as a sort of decoration for the person of the
Founder. ' Hegel . . . held that the believer operates with figura-
tive conceptions, the philosopher with exact notions, supposing
that thereby he had brought the two into perfect harmony ;
Strauss for pictorial thinking put mythology, and so dug " the
ugly ditch " between the two deeper than ever.'[1] The origins
of Christianity he finds not in a Person but in an idea. He argues
that if any narrative expresses for a religious body its basis then
ipso facto that narrative is a myth. Since myths only develop with
time the Gospel narratives can in no sense be said to rest upon the
testimony of eye-witnesses. Strauss makes it perfectly clear that
he is working on the basis of the Hegelian philosophy, of whose
truth he was absolutely convinced. Because he accepted the
Hegelian dialectic he rejected outright the assumption that the
initiator of a process could be the greatest of that development.
The unique place which faith accords to Jesus Christ cannot be
occupied by him or any other one man. The true God-Man is not
a man but humanity as a whole. What Christian faith says of Jesus
Christ should be said of the race as a whole.

' Mankind is the unity of the two natures, the Infinite
Spirit depotentiated in finitude, and the finite spirit mindful
of its infinity ; it is the child of the visible mother and the
invisible father, of Spirit and nature ; it is the miracle-worker,
for in the course of human history the spirit ever more fully
takes control of nature ; it is the Sinless One, for its progres-
sive growth is blameless, and impunity clings only to the
single life but disappears in the race ; it is the Dying, Rising
and Ascending One, for from the negation of its merely
natural qualities there springs an ever higher spiritual life,

[1] H. R. Mackintosh, op. cit., p. 118.

and through the abrogation of its finitude as personal, national and secular spirit it is exalted into unity with the Infinite Spirit of heaven.'[1]

What then is the significance of Jesus Christ? The answer is what Hegel had said before—Jesus was the first to perceive that God and man are one. Later the Church changed this idea into the dogma that God and man are one—in Jesus Christ. Clearly Strauss reached his conclusions not by any sort of examination of the data but simply because they were the logical outcome of his Hegelian premises.

Such was the progress of Hegelianism in Germany. The Hegelian philosophy was, however, very influential outside of Germany and particularly in the Scandinavian countries. We shall now briefly examine the development of philosophy and theology in Denmark in the opening years of the nineteenth century. As we have suggested already, the philosophical movement in Denmark was largely an appropriation on the part of certain philosophers of Hegelian ideas. Høffding points out that those who were most interested in these ideas were ' students of Aesthetics and theologians '.[2] It was Johan Ludwig Heiberg (1791–1860) who first introduced Hegel's philosophy into Denmark. He had studied under Hegel himself in Berlin and had come into personal contact with the Master. He returned from Berlin with the basic ideas of the System clear and complete in his mind. All his life Heiberg held fast to these basic ideas and he was convinced that only this System could produce unity of the spiritual life, and particularly Art and Religion could only be seen properly in its light. Heiberg's first appearance on the scene of European philosophy was in 1824 when he published in Kiel his *Ueber Menschliche Freiheit* to which he was provoked by the determinism of Howitz. Later it was aesthetic subjects more especially which gave him occasion to apply the new philosophy. Høffding calls him the apostle of Hegelianism in Denmark,[3] and a contemporary historian says of him :

' He was considered throughout Denmark a man of great powers of mind and extensive erudition. . . . Heiberg

---

[1] Quoted by Mackintosh, op. cit., p. 119.
[2] Høffding, *History of Modern Philosophy*, vol. ii, p. 285.
[3] Høffding, *Søren Kierkegaard, som filosof.*, p. 16.

considers (the system of Hegel) the most profound and philosophic of any which Germany has produced.'[1]

Heiberg regarded Hegel's System as presenting essentially the same outlook on life as Goethe had put forward in his poetry, and he was quite impressed by the fact that there was this agreement between the two great intellects of the modern Germany. In 1837 he proceeded to show the relevance of the new philosophy to theology by publishing a book on ' the doctrine of the Trinity ' (Treenighedslaeren). He also developed the Hegelian interpretation of Logic in a series of lectures which he gave in the Military High School some of which he then published in the periodical he began called *Perseus*.

In an essay ' On the Importance of Philosophy for their Time ' Heiberg had said that there was an overcrowding of ideas. Compared with art, poetry and religion, now scientific and political ideas were asserting themselves more and more. But in which order, in what reciprocal relation should all these ideas and interests stand to each other? Here we reach a decision only by a comparison of the different fundamental ideas. But the age does not always offer a manifold of ideas so much as an one-sidedness. A particular idea or interest, for example political or religious, will set itself up as the highest and decisive. No idea or interest was really significant, each contributing the complement of the other, and only life as a whole, the synthesis of Truth, shows where each has its place. In this way we are led to philosophy which is the thorough study of these fundamental ideas in their mutual relation. Philosophy describes the connection between the world of ideas and Truth.

Just as for Hegel so for Heiberg, Philosophy and Religion have the same content—only the form is different. The absolute (God) appears in the latter in the form of a representation, that is imaginatively, whereas in the case of the former it appears as a concept. One reaches Paradise by two ways—either by becoming absorbed in the historical form of Christ or by having speculatively apprehended God. Only the latter is a satisfactory way, and to it we must return again and again, if Religion is to

[1] Robert Blakey, *History of the Philosophy of Mind*, London, Trelawney Wm. Saunders, 1848.

have validity. Only what can be put in conceptual form is valid. Philosophy does not prove God's existence, which simply cannot be proved, but it makes the representation of God which it is given into the Idea of God. In the Christian doctrine of the Trinity Heiberg finds an agreement with Hegel's philosophy. ' The constant trilogy going through the Hegelian System is itself a reflection of the Trinity in Thought's, Nature's and Spirit's empires and the absolute beginning for all philosophy.'

When in 1841 Heiberg published his 'Prose Writings' (*Prosaisk Skrifter*) he recalled in the Introduction how the Hegelian philosophy had been resisted by the academic world. They neglected it or put it in quarantine. But he rejoiced at the thought that it had now become the fashion and by the vigorous work of a youthful genius was *causa victrix*. This young worker in the field of culture to whom Heiberg referred was Hans Lassen Martensen (1808–1884) who had lectured on speculative theology and philosophy in the University of Copenhagen and had won great praise. In his student years Martensen had been greatly taken up with Hegel and felt himself powerfully drawn to it. He was particularly enthusiastic about the prospect that Hegel's Philosophy gave speculative theology, which could stand as a higher unity against Rationalism and Orthodoxy. The great ideal of his youth he himself expressed in these words : ' There must be a view of life and of the world in which everything that has meaning in existence (*Dasein*)—nature and spirit, nature and history, poetry and art and philosophy harmoniously unite to form a temple of the spirit in which Christianity is the all-governing and all-explaining centre.'[1] Such a view he thought he could find with the assistance of Hegelian philosophy. For the Hegelian philosophy seemed to open up the possibility of divine knowledge and so afforded a basis for theology. It might be thought that Schleiermacher had pointed out the way the theologian must go, but the defect of his work was that he had left all the speculative problems untouched. The speculative spirit of the young theologian was not going to be suffocated by the old master, and so he turned to Hegel. He wanted to construct a philosophy on the basis given in the imaginative language of positive religion. He did not indeed want to be slavish in his allegiance to Hegel and

[1] Martensen, *Af Mit Livnet*, p. 23.

insisted that he would not follow the abstract logical method the master had used. The ideal that the great man had before him, however, would be his too : to reconcile Faith and Knowledge. He saw that for Hegel dogma was really only a symbol, and though he did not reject this he was not anxious to replace images with concepts. In fact his aim was to unite mysticism and the Hegelian theory of religious thought as imagery. His heroes were the old philosophers and mystics, and he wanted to follow in the footsteps of Meister Eckhardt and Jacob Böhme. He did not want ' to move away from the image to come to the concept but, on the contrary, to clarify the image by means of the concept, to present a unity of the concept and the intuition.' This is definitely the aim of his *Christian Dogmatics* which at first glance seems quite without fault. Some quotations will serve to make this clear.

> ' The δos που στω, so often expressed by an inquiring philosophy, is for dogmatic theology answered at once ; the theologian does not seek to make the truth depend on his investigation, but only seeks to gain by his thought a firmer grasp of the truth which he already accepts as fully certain, and at which he first arrived in quite another way than that of speculation.'[1]

> ' The task of dogmatic theology, therefore, is to set forth Christian views in the form of a connected doctrinal system. This process is primarily an *explicative* one, that is, its first business is to unfold the elements contained in Christian intuition, to develop the inner connection existing between them. But we cannot undertake to explain or unfold without feeling also the impulse to speculate or comprehend ; in other words, we cannot be content merely with exhibiting the connection between the various parts of what we find given to our hand, but we desire also to understand the why and wherefore . . . and the essential feature of speculation is to reconcile antagonism in the higher units of the idea.'[2]

We see then that Martensen was the real Danish Hegelian and that Kierkegaard did him no injustice when he caricatured

[1] Martensen, *Christian Dogmatics*, p. 3.
[2] ibid., p. 65. Cp. pp. 67 ff.

him as ' the professor ' and said that the Hegelians had dissolved faith down to nothing. His thought and that of the master and the other disciples make up the background, the climate of opinion prevailing in Denmark in the eighteen hundreds. Against this we are to see the great challenge that Truth is Subjectivity.

CHAPTER III

THE PRINCIPLE OF SUBJECTIVITY

Our very first task in dealing with this theme is to justify our assumption that it is the fundamental part of Kierkegaard's whole treatment of faith. Not all the scholars are agreed on this, and they differ considerably in their estimate of the importance they attach to it. For instance, in the introductory chapter to his voluminous book, *Kierkegaard's Dogmatiska Åskådning*,[1] Bohlin admits that in his teaching of Christianity Kierkegaard strongly emphasised that from a religious point of view the decisive thing is a how and not a what. In his analysis of Kierkegaard's work, however, Bohlin would distinguish sharply between two trends of thought which he believes are to be found in Kierkegaard's interpretation of Christianity. One of these, he argues, represents Kierkegaard's own experience, whereas the other is only an artificial construction, intended simply as a weapon to defeat his speculative opponents, but quite foreign to his real understanding of Christianity. So Bohlin maintains that the questions of faith and sin are answered in a double way. Without being aware of it, Kierkegaard advocated two different conceptions of sin. One conception is dominant in *The Concept of Dread* and *The Sickness unto Death*, the other in *Philosophical Fragments* and the *Concluding Unscientific Postscript*. Bohlin's contention, then, is that Kierkegaard wrote the former two books from his personal experience of sin and freedom, of the unapproachable mystery of the numinous, and this is why in these two books he can recognise at one and the same time the reality of moral freedom and the unconquerable power of sin. On the other hand, in the *Fragments* and in the *Postscript*, the idea of sin is intellectualistically determined, and sin is regarded as a paradoxical transformation of the human reason which is one with his nature. Now, in *The Concept of Dread* and *The Sickness unto Death* faith is represented simply as the opposite of sin, that is to say, as communion with God; whereas, in the *Fragments* and the *Postscript*, on the other hand, faith is identified with the belief that Christ was God and Man.

[1] Torsten Bohlin, *Kierkegaard's Dogmatiska Åskådning*, Stockholm, 1925.

Bohlin does indeed admit that the mere theoretical recognition of the dual nature does not suffice to constitute what is there called faith, but he insists that it is strictly necessary. In these writings, therefore, the concept of faith is deduced from the idea of Christianity as a contrast to speculation, as the absolute paradox.

> ' Thus the analysis of the fundamental determination of faith in Kierkegaard ends in the result that it is two altogether different conceptions of faith that clash, one of which is theoretically determined while the other is in a special sense christocentrically determined, and the former of which belongs to the personally religious line of experience, while the other goes back to a marked view of the special nature of Christianity as opposed to other theological trends.'[1]

The inadequacy of this theory of Bohlin's becomes apparent when we examine his method. He establishes his position by analysis of islolated passages taken from the different works. So he claims to have demonstrated this marked lack of agreement in Kierkegaard's production which reveals itself as an inner contrast between two opposed aspects of his teachings on the nature of faith. Lindström rightly argues that both Bohlin's procedure and his results are wrong, insisting that the question of Kierkegaard's theological and moral views cannot be treated as isolated problems at all. Rather they must be seen against the background of his general view. Now, we are no more anxious to follow Lindström in all respects than we are to follow Bohlin, but it is clear that his contention here is very justified. Bohlin assumes without attempting to substantiate his claim that one idea expresses personal experience and the other does not. If his theory were correct the theme of subjectivity could be shown to have no relation at all to previous theology and philosophy. But we shall see that not only the idea of Paradox which he rejects as being a deliberate attempt to answer Hegel but also that of subjectivity derives from German anti-Hegelian philosophy amongst other things. For these reasons we would say that Bohlin's theory constitutes an unwarranted and unjust interpretation of Kierkegaard. It ignores the coherence and consistency of Kierke-

[1] Bohlin, op. cit., pp. 254-5.

gaard's thought, denying its real, if complex, unity. We feel that Lindström is on much safer ground when he says :

> ' The main principle . . . must be to try to understand Kierkegaard's world of thought as a unitary view. In the case of the apparent contradictions the question must always be put whether a defining of the meaning of the concepts in the judgments which apparently are at variance may not solve the difficulties. In the case of a man of Kierkegaard's standard we must quite simply take it for granted that seemingly opposed tendencies are in some way held together by a general view. . . . A unitary total view must therefore be assumed which forms the background of, and is reflected in, the edifying writings as well as the aesthetic productions.'[1]

Emmanuel Hirsch is another scholar who has argued strongly for the totality view against the piecemeal view which Bohlin represents. The wider sense of the totality-view does not preclude the relation between Kierkegaard's biography and the development of his thought. The advantage of this view is that it enables us to look at these two themes of subjectivity and paradox as related. According to Bohlin, the theme of paradox is an artificial construction ; but the truth of the matter is that it can hardly be called more artificial or less integral to Kierkegaard's thought than the subjectivity theme, and is indeed clearly the counterpart of it. Lindström makes more or less this very point :

> ' The ethical cannot be grasped by man, except in a concrete situation and at a particular moment, and he cannot be possessed of the truth in any other way than through a decision by action ; *subjectivity is the truth. The counterpart of this thesis is that the truth objectively determined is a paradox.'*[2]

This interconnection of the two themes which we are discussing is very obvious in the *Postscript* and also in other works.[3] Surely this is proof enough of the injustice which Bohlin's view does to Kierkegaard's argument. Yet, despite the fact that we

[1] Valter Lindström, *Stadiernas Teologi*, Lund, 1943, pp. 10–11.
[2] ibid., p. 233. (italics mine).
[3] Vide *Postscript*, pp. 45, 191–2, 288, 290. Cp. *Fear and Trembling*, pp. 76, 81 ff, 100. *Fragments*, pp. 39 ff. *Training in Christianity*, pp. 143 ff.

regard the way in which Bohlin has interpreted Kierkegaard as
wrong it is clear that he too is quite definite on the point that
this theme of subjectivity is of fundamental importance in what
Kierkegaard has to say about faith. In the same way Dr. H. V.
Martin says very properly :

> ' Kierkegaard's thesis that Truth is subjectivity is at once
> the most important for the understanding of his polemic
> against philosophical interpretations of Christianity, and at
> the same time the most difficult to understand without mis-
> conception.'[1]

Now that we have grasped the importance of this idea of
subjectivity in Kierkegaard let us try and make clear what influences can be said to have led him to this position. For original
though he was, Kierkegaard did not arrive at this position without
the influence and guidance of previous thinkers. First, it is only
natural to expect that Luther was amongst these, and that he
was an influence seems to us hardly dubitable. We must admit
that he probably influenced Kierkegaard more by the movement
or Church of which he was the father than by his actual works.[2]
There has been no discussion in English of this rather tricky
point apart from the very brief comments in M. Regis Jolivet's
Introduction to Kierkegaard.[3] The English translation of the *Journals*
enables us to see the great interest Kierkegaard took in him during
his later years ; but this is of no use whatsoever in deciding
what influence Luther had on his development. M. Jolivet points
out the similarity between Kierkegaard and Luther, and would
seem to suggest that Luther is one of the great formative influences
on Kierkegaard.[4] This we must doubt, though here again scholars
are not agreed. Niels Thulstrup, the Secretary of the Kierkegaard
Society, a leading Kierkegaard scholar, says that Luther had
practically no influence on Kierkegaard's philosophy of subjectivity. On the other hand, Prof. Valter Lindström claims that
Luther had a considerable influence on Kierkegaard, a view shared

---

[1] H. V. Martin, *Kierkegaard the Melancholy Dane*, Epworth Press 1950, p. 43.
[2] Prof. Cornelio Fabro, the Italian translator of Kierkegaard agrees with me on
this point. In a letter to me he says : ' The influence of Luther as far as we can judge
from the *Papirer* is indirect. It comes from the Protestant milieu which surrounded
Kierkegaard.'
[3] R. Jolivet, *Introduction to Kierkegaard*, Muller, London, 1950, pp. 206–19.
[4] ibid., pp. 206–8.

by M. Jean Wahl. Now the difficulty with Mr. Thulstrup's contention is that it cannot explain the surprising points of similarity between Luther and Kierkegaard; while Prof. Lindström of course admits that it was only in 1846 that Kierkegaard began reading Luther seriously, as is indeed quite clear from the *Papirer*. The Principle of Subjectivity is quite clearly stated in the *Postscript* which was published in 1845. In this work there are only two references to Luther, neither of which is important.[1] M. Jolivet rightly says that there are many ideas which are common to them both, such as the notion of sin as the opposite of faith, and the idea of faith as ' the leap into the absurd '. How, then, are we to explain this if Luther had no influence on Kierkegaard? The answer may well be that Kierkegaard absorbed Luther in ideas from text-books.[2] This must be very probably because such books were widely read at the time. There is also a passage in Luther's *Greater Catechism* which seems to us very much like the way in which Kierkegaard illustrates his Principle of Subjectivity in the *Postscript*.

' What means it to have a God? Or what is God? Answer : God is one from whom we can expect all good and in whom we can take refuge for all our needs, so that to have a God is nothing else than to trust in him with all our hearts ; as I have often said, that trust and faith of the heart alone make both God and Idol. If thy faith and thy trust are right, then thy God is also the right God, and again if thy trust is false and wrong, then thou hast not the right God. For the two, faith and God hold close together. Whatever then thy heart clings to (I say) and relies upon, that is properly thy God.'[3]

This bears a striking resemblance to Kierkegaard's parable about the Christian and the pagan.[4]

---

[1] *Postscript*, pp. 145, 304.

[2] On the evidence of *Papirer* II A 434, we would say that he had been reading Lutheran Theology. There is a reference to ' certain dogmatists ', who, according to the editors of the *Papirer*, are K. G. Brettschneider and Karl August von Hase. The former's *Handbuch der Dogmatik der evangelisch-Lutherischen Kirche* was published in Leipzig in 1838 and the latter's *Hutterus Redivivus oder Dogmatik der evangelisch-Lutherischen Kirche* two years before in Leipzig also.' Both these works are listed in the sale catalogue of Kierkegaard's library, *Fortegnelse over Dr. Søren A. Kierkegaard's efterladte Bogsamling*, København 1856, being items.

[3] Luther, *Catechismus Major*, Luther's *Primary Works*. Hodder and Stoughton, London, 1896, p. 34.   [4] *Postscript*, p. 179.

For Luther religion was not something complicated but something quite simple ; not something dependent on external agents and intermediaries, but something altogether spiritual, personal, inward, not a state of knowledge but a state of mind, a *Gesinnung*, which the believer first experiences personally as serenity of conscience. This state of feeling presupposes a knowledge which can only be gained by the individual through personal experience. To seek God, and find Him ; to fear, love and trust God above all things, to let the heart rest on God alone—this to Luther is the whole of religion.[1] This emphasis on a ' spiritual ' religion of the heart can have contributed to Kierkegaard's development of his Principle of Subjectivity. Certainly in so far as this is regarded as a finely religious thing it seems difficult to distinguish them. Perhaps our strongest argument is that Kierkegaard himself said that they were the same,

> ' Formally the category of ' for thee ' (Subjectivity, Inwardness) with which *Either-Or* ended (only the truth that edifies is truth for thee) is exactly Luther's.'[2]

Yet even this is insufficient for in the same passage Kierkegaard says he has never really learnt anything from Luther.

While the influence of Luther on Kierkegaard can be said to be an open question, that of Franz Von Baader is hardly so. Yet there has been barely any mention of him in discussions of the sources of Kierkegaard's thought. Von Baader[3] has been regarded as a disciple of Schelling, and is listed by Ueberweg in his *History* as such.[4] However, it is the opinion of most scholars that Schelling was indebted to Baader and possibly owed the mystical elements of his later work to him. Certainly, as the *Encyclopaedia Britannica* says, there was a ' mutual influence ' between them.[5] They were both amongst the foremost in the revolt against Hegelianism,

---

[1] Cp. E. Bréhier, *Histoire de la Philosophie Allemande*, Paris 1921, pp. 14–16.
[2] *Papirer*, VII A. 465.
[3] Franz Xaver Von Baader (1765–1841) was born at Munich, studied medicine and later became a mining engineer. While in England (1792–6) he was introduced to mysticism by Boehme. On his return to Hamburg he became acquainted with Jacobi and Schelling and became very friendly with Schelling. From 1817–20 he was Superintendent of Bavarian mines, but in 1826 he was appointed professor of Philosophy and Theology at Munich.
[4] Ueberweg, *History of Philosophy*, London, 1874, vol. II, p. 226.
[5] *Encyclopaedia Britannica* (14th Edition), vol. II, p. 833.

which took place in German philosophy during the early part of the nineteenth century. It is likely then that Kierkegaard's Principle of Subjectivity was a deliberate continuation of the struggle against Hegel which Von Baader and others initiated. To support this contention with chapter and verse is difficult indeed, but it can be supported. There are several references to Von Baader in Kierkegaard's writings.[1] It might be argued that this evidence is too slight to show any influence, but this is to ignore the fact that Von Baader had made a contribution to the anti-Hegelian movement which was quite similar to that which we have in Kierkegaard. Von Baader had two important things to say. The first is that we can never know God or know about Him even, without God Himself. The radical error of rational theology is that it assumes the contrary. As Eckhardt had said, however, the eye through which God sees us is the same as that in which I see Him, since it is one and the same thing to be known of God and to know Him. The second point is an even clearer criticism of Hegel. He says that Hegel is wrong in regarding God as an object of our reason since He is absolute Spirit. The agreement between this and Kierkegaard's thesis that God is infinite subjectivity and is known only in subjectivity is obvious. It would be foolish to say that Baader is the source of this, but it would surely be equally foolish to say that there is no connection between them.

Schelling was a much more important influence, and the nature and extent of his influence has not been fully studied by anyone. There is ample evidence, however, both in the *Works* and the *Papers*. There are some references to him in the *Journals*, in *The Concept of Dread*, and the *Postscript* and a veiled reference in the *Philosophical Fragments*.[2] The reference in the *Fragments* is of little importance and is in fact nothing more than the use of one of Schelling's terms.[3] Again, the critical remarks in the *Postscript* give us little evidence of the importance Schelling had for

[1] In the *Samlede Værker* the references are the following: IV 272, 344, 364, XII 345, the first three of which are to be seen in the English translations (*Philosophical Fragments*, p. 9, *The Concept of Dread*, pp. 36, 53). The references in the *Papirer* are: I A 174, C 27, II A 7, A 31, C 14, C 34. Only the first is in translation—Journals 61.

[2] The references are *Journals*, 392, 399, 868 ; *Concept of Dread*, pp. 11, 12, 19, 28 53f, 102, 121 ; *Fragments*, p. 65 ; *Postscript*, pp. 96, 134 n., 299. In the *Samlede Værker* they are IV, 315, 317, 325, 334, 364 f., 422, 445 ; *VII*, 93, 135, 324.

[3] Vide *Fragments*, p. 65, and Prof. Swenson's note on p. 103 on 'construction'.

Kierkegaard. Indeed, if one is to see the relation between the two we must search for our evidence in Kierkegaard's work and papers before 1842. When he was in Berlin in 1841 he notes in his *Journal* :

> ' I am so pleased to have heard Schelling's second lecture, indescribably. I have sighed for long enough and my thoughts have sighed within me ; when he mentioned the word " reality " in connection with the relation of philosophers to reality the fruit of my thought leapt for joy within me as in Elizabeth. I remember almost every word he said from that moment on. Here perhaps is the dawning of truth. That one word reminded me of all my philosophic sufferings and pains. . . . Now I have put all my hopes in Schelling.'[1]

However, his hopes were doomed to disappointment. By February he had stopped going to the lectures and on February 27th, 1842, he wrote to his brother Peter, ' Schelling drivels on intolerably '.

Yet in this very letter where he describes in most biting terms his disgust with Schelling and his lectures, he admits that the fact that Schelling was lecturing in Berlin was what made him go there.[2] This and the references in the *Journals* of the preceding years provide the evidence for saying that Kierkegaard regarded Schelling as being something of a guide in his search for a philosophical position.[3] It was probably Schelling's later philosophy that attracted Kierkegaard, and if we consider this briefly we shall see the relation between them. In 1834 Schelling published a preface to Hubert Becker's translation of a work by Victor Cousin.[4] Here he described the Hegelian philosophy as being merely negative, as substituting for the real and the loving a logical concept devoid of all empirical elements, and, by a most singular fiction or hypostatization, ascribing to the concept the power of self-motion, which belongs only to that for which the concept was substituted. In the Munich lectures on the *History of Modern Philosophy*[5] Schelling makes a similar point with

---

[1] *Journals* 392. (*Papirer* III A 179).
[2] *Journals* 399. (*Papirer* III A 195).
[3] He started reading Schelling in 1837 (Vide II A 31).
[4] *Fragments Philosophiques*, Paris, 1833 ; Schelling, *Werke* I 10, pp. 201 f.
[5] Schelling, *Werke*, vol. I 10, pp. 1–201.

regard to such abstract concepts as being, existence, and so on. He argues that the abstract presupposes that from which they are abstracted, that these concepts exist only in the mind and so are not prior to nature, their condition, nor can they have any power which would make them part of Nature. The lectures to which we saw Kierkegaard refer above must have been a continuation of the *Inaugural Lecture at Berlin* which was published in 1841 and which we know was in Kierkegaard's library.[1] Here Schelling said that he did not reject the discovery of his youth, the Principle of Identity, which Hegel had reduced to a mere abstraction, a matter of logic. However, his acceptance of it was determined by what he called positive philosophy which was to supplement this negative philosophy. Positive philosophy will by means of experience advance beyond rational science and is distinguished by being the philosophy of Mythology and Revelation. ' Schelling ' says Høffding ' insisted very strongly on the fact that speculative philosophy could not escape from the possible and the abstract and that the relation to absolute reality of which religious belief laid hold could only be regarded as an act of will which proceeds from aspiration and practical and personal need (as Kierkegaard says ' from a leap '). He goes on to suggest that Schelling's presentation of the opposition of thought and existence, of the impossibility of continuous movement was something Kierkegaard never abandoned.[2] Positive philosophy, according to Schelling, does not seek to prove the existence of God from the idea of God, but rather, setting out with the facts of existence, to prove the divinity of the existent. As Erdmann puts it, whilst the negative philosophy had God for its goal the positive philosophy has God as its principle.[3] It will be in fact a philosophy of revelation precisely because it is a philosophy of reality and of the religious reality. Since God is its principle it will be a philosophy founded on history which will be interpreted not as necessary evolution but as the expression of the will of God.[4] These Berlin lectures were published by Schelling's

---

[1] *Schellings erste Vorlesung in Berlin*, Stuttgart and Tübingen 1841 is item 767 of *Fortegnelse over Dr. Søren A Kierkegaard Bogsamling*. It is interesting that items 763-7 are all works of Schelling.

[2] Harold Høffding, *Kierkegaard som filosof*, p. 58.

[3] Erdmann, *History of Philosophy*, III, p. 173.

[4] Schelling, *Werke*, II pp. 4, 11 ff., 164, 174, 175.

pupils from class-notes in 1842, and also posthumously in his Collected Works. But there is a manuscript in the Kierkegaard archive in the Royal Library in Copenhagen which contains the notes Kierkegaard took of Schelling's lectures.[1] An extremely important point about the positive philosophy which must have attracted Kierkegaard was Schelling's insistence that it assumes a real relation between man and God. For Schelling the real relation between God and Men is between the *individual* and God, and there is thus only an indirect (or more correctly a theoretical or abstract) relation between God and humanity.[2] An equally significant point was the importance of choice for Schelling and his contention that positive philosophy is a philosophy that makes room for freedom.[3] The marked similarity between Schelling's positive philosophy and Kierkegaard's anti-Hegelian position when taken together with the historical details we have mentioned is evidence enough of the direct influence Schelling had on Kierkegaard.

Schelling's influence, however, was not as great as that of Johan Georg Hamann, ' The Magus of the North ', described by Dr. Walter Lowrie as the most important single influence on Kierkegaard.[4] Hamann (1730–1788) was a firm opponent of the eighteenth-century Enlightenment in Germany. His work is little known, mainly because it is completely unsystematic, indeed chaotic, and written in a tortuous and difficult style. In his very first work which he called *The Memorabilia of Socrates*, he opposed his standpoint of faith to the rationalism of Enlightenment and the philosophy of Kant. His contention quite simply is that belief is more important than knowledge and understanding.

' Our own existence and the existence of all objects without us must be believed, and can in no other way be

---

[1] Vide *Papirer* III C 27—' Kollegie til Schellings Forelaesninger i Berlin ' Kierkegaard Arkivet C Pk 4 Laeg. 4.

[2] Schelling, *Werke*, II pp. 1, 556, 566, 569.

[3] Cf. Ruttenbeck, *Søren Kierkegaard Der Christliche Denker und sein Werke*, 1929, p. 78.

[4] Vide Lowrie, op. cit., p. 164. ' I am inclined to say that he is the only author by whom Søren Kierkegaard was profoundly influenced.' Cf. Lowrie, *Hamann*, Princeton 1951. Hamann was born at Königsberg on August 17th, 1730, of poor parents. In 1767 he was made translator in the civil service, and ten years later he became a storekeeper in a mercantile house. He was dismissed with a small pension about 1784. He was extremely poor but friends made it possible for him to spend some time away from Königsberg. He died on June 21st, 1788.

made out. . . . What a man believes, therefore, does not
need to be proved, and a proposition may be proved ever
so incontrovertibly without on that account being believed.
Faith is no operation of the Reason, and cannot therefore
be defeated by any attack from the side of Reason, because
faith comes as little through argument as tasting or seeing.'[1]

These remarks illustrate at once the power and the confusion
to be seen in Hamann. They also are of very much the same
flavour as Kierkegaard's writing. It is difficult to say clearly what
Hamann's point is here if only because of the ambiguity of the
term ' belief '. Belief can mean the acceptance of a hypothesis
on evidence which is considerable but not demonstrative, or it
can be used to mean the acceptance of an assertion without any
reason being given. Hamann's point is then that in order that
a man should hold a certain view it is not necessary that the truth
of this be demonstrable. From this he moves to the position
that faith is something different from Reason and is best thought
of as an immediate awareness like sight. He argues then that
intellectual reflection and faith are quite different because the
certainty of the latter is not the certainty of a demonstration.
As a protest against the one-sided rationalism of his day, which
would include within itself all that was contained in religion,
this protest was quite sound and justifiable. However, the protest
became a dogma for Hamann, and his insight led him to a deep
hatred of all philosophical systems which he regarded as the
spider's web woven by vanity. Indeed the only value he attached
to philosophy is the negative one of being the instrument by
means of which science is discredited. Thus philosophy becomes
a strange sort of paedogogus to lead us to positive faith. Faith
itself has nothing to do with philosophy. This is the theme of
a somewhat long passage which is worth quoting nonetheless
because of its power and its vigorous style.

' Our salvation depends as little upon conformity to
reason or correctness of belief as genius does upon diligence,
or good fortune upon merit. Since faith is one of the natural
conditions of our faculties of knowledge and the funda-

---

[1] Quoted by Pfleiderer, *The Philosophy of Religion*, London, 1886, vol. I, p. 197

mental impulse of our souls ; since every universal proposition rests upon good faith, and all abstractions are and must
be arbitrary, the most celebrated thinkers of our time upon
religion divest themselves of their premises and middle
terms, which are necessary to the demonstration of rational
conclusions. The basis of religion lies in our whole existence,
and outside the sphere of our powers of knowledge, which
all taken together compose the most accidental and abstract
mode of our existence. Hence that mythical and poetical
vein in all religions, their foolishness and irritating form in
the eyes of an alien, incompetent, ice-cold and starved
philosophy.'[1]

The great number of references to Hamann in Kierkegaard's
writings is proof enough of his profound influence.[2] It was in
the autumn of 1835 that Kierkegaard became acquainted with
Hamann's writings—that is, just at the time when he had come
to the conclusion that Christianity and philosophy could not be
reconciled and so Christianity was an untenable position.[3] As
we have already seen, it was as a result of reading Hamann that
he abandoned this position. Hamann taught him an important
thing which he was never to forget and was in fact to make his
own position, one which he developed, and this was that faith's
certainty can never be destroyed by a philosophical attack because
it is not ' an operation of Reason '. In this connection we recall
that he was particularly impressed by Hamann's comment that
Hume's criticism and doubts were but proof of the proposition
he attacked. The passage from Hume in question is this from the
Enquiry :

' The Christian religion . . . cannot be believed by any
reasonable person without a miracle. Mere reason is insufficient to convince us of its veracity ; and whosoever is

---

[1] Quoted by Pfleiderer, op. cit. vol. I, p. 199.
[2] Kierkegaard's reference to Hamann in the translated works are these : *Either-
Or* I. *Fear and Trembling* motto after title page ; *Repetition*, p. 34 f ; *Stages upon
Life's Way*, pp. 100, 111, 122, 138, 146, 187 ; *Concept of Dread*, pp. 85, 145 n ; *Fragments*, p. 42 f ; *Postscript*, pp. 223 f., 258 n., 495 ; *Journals* 121, 141, 196, 404, 695.
The Danish references are : *Vaerker* I 253, III 66, 212 f., IV 245, 246, 302, 306, 402,
474, V 54, VI 104, 109, 117, 130, 149, 159, 206, VII 236, 377, 549. *Papirer* I A 100,
237, 340, II A 2, 12, 75, 102, 105, 114, 118, 136, 138, 259, 438, 442.
[3] *Journals* 32 (I A 99).

moved by faith to assent to it, is conscious of a continued miracle in his own person which subverts all the principles of understanding, and gives him a determination to believe what is most contrary to custom and experience.[1]

It is clear that by his attack on reason and his emphasis on the primacy of belief, his definition of faith as different from reason Hamann contributed to Kierkegaard's development of his Principle of Subjectivity. We would emphasise here, however, that Kierkegaard's admiration did not lead to a slavish imitation, and his use of Hamann shows a coherence lacking in Hamann himself.[2]

Yet another thinker must be mentioned as a powerful influence on Kierkegaard—he is Lessing. If Hamann is, as Lowrie says, the greatest influence on Kierkegaard, Lessing must be admitted to come second. Significantly enough Fulford, who probably had never read Kierkegaard's Papers and wrote from his knowledge of the Works, says : ' From Lessing and (later) Schopenhauer among foreigners . . . he apparently learnt most.'[3] Mr. Mesnard remarks that it is somewhat surprising to see Lessing quoted in the *Postscript* since Lessing was not a particularly religous thinker.[4] But Kierkegaard explained his admiration of Lessing in the *Postscript* :

' My admiration of Lessing has to do with . . . the fact that he religiously shut himself up within the isolation of his own subjectivity ; that he did not allow himself to be deceived into becoming world-historic and systematic with respect to the religions, but understood and knew how to hold fast to the understanding that the religions concerned Lessing, and Lessing alone, just as it concerned every other human being in the same manner ; understood that he had infinitely to do with God, and nothing, nothing to do with any man directly. This is my theme, the object of my gratitude.'[5]

---

[1] David Hume, *Essays Moral, Political and Literary*, ed. Green and Grose, London, 1875, vol. II, p. 108. Cp. I A 237.
[2] Cp. *Journals* 40 (I A 123) : ' Hamann makes an observation which I can use, *although he neither understood it as I wish to nor thought more about it* . . .' (italics mine).
[3] F. W. Fulford, op. cit., p. 3. The references in the *Vaerker* are : I 166, 169, IV 172, 177 f., 399, VI 407, 460 ,VII 28, 51 ff., 79, 94, 103, 109, VII 161, XIII 378.
[4] Mesnard, op. cit. p. 301.   [5] *Postscript*, p. 61.

Lessing (1729–1782) was a critic and a dramatist, but since his student days he had been interested in philosophy, and the last years of his life were devoted chiefly to theological controversy. However, as far back as 1751, in his prose introduction to *Die Religion* Lessing had shown that he had broken with the philosophy of the Enlightenment. He speaks of the labyrinths of ' *Selbst-kenntnis* ' and maintains that self-examination has always been and will be the first and safest path to religion. This Socratic stand-point is made even more Socratic by the mixture of seriousness and humour in Lessing.[1] All this Kierkegaard lays up in his mind as it were :

> ' No indeed Lessing was no serious man. His entire mode of communication is without earnestness, being lacking in that true dependability which suffices for . . . those who always think in the wake of someone else, though without thoughtfulness.'[2]

So true is this indeed that when one looks for the results of Lessing's thought one discovers that there are none. This delights Kierkegaard very much.[3] For this illustrates how completely erroneous the System is when it seeks to embody within it Lessing and his work. In the eyes of the Hegelian systematiser, ' to be sure, Lessing has long since been left behind ; he is merely a vanishing little way-station on the systematic railway of world history '.[4] Yet if what Lessing has said is true then ' it would seem a little questionable to run away from it so fast, with the speed of a railway train '.[5] This way of considering the search for truth as being as important as the truth is directly connected with the thesis Kierkegaard maintained, that subjectivity is truth. This is very clear from the *Postscript* where the expressions of glowing admiration leave us in no doubt about the importance of Lessing for Kierkegaard.[6] So congenial does Kierkegaard find him in fact that he thinks he can well afford to develop his theme by stating ' theses possibly or actually attributable to Lessing.'[7]

Lessing's influence is seen again when Kierkegaard once more discusses the problem he had formulated in the *Fragments*.[8] In his pamphlet written in answer to Göze, chief pastor of Hamburg,

[1] *Postscript*, p. 65. [2] ibid., p. 64. [3] ibid., p. 61.
[4] ibid., p. 63. [5] ibid., p. 63. [6] *Postscript*, pp. 61–66.
[7] ibid., p. 67. [8] ibid., pp. 345 f.

Lessing raises the question of the relation of history to the truth of a religion. In other words, can a religion be said to be true which rests on certain historical traditions? Historical arguments always rest upon the credibility of external witnesses; but even the best authenticated can never yield more than a high degree of probability. Therefore they can never give us the certainty on which we would rest our salvation. He takes the miracles as an instance and discusses the significance of their historical truth, if that is assumed, for our religious faith:

' What is meant by believing a historical truth? Surely nothing more than to acquiesce in it, to have nothing to urge against it, to be satisfied that another person should build upon it another historical statement. If I . . . have nothing to urge from a historical point of view against the statement that Jesus Christ raised a man from the dead, must I therefore hold it proved that God has a Son who is of like nature with himself? From the former historical truth to make a leap into quite another kind of truth and to require of me to reconstruct all my metaphysical and moral ideas in accordance therewith; to bid me, because I cannot oppose any creditable witness to the resurrection of Christ, alter my fundamental ideas about the nature of Deity to suit it—if that is not a μεταβασις εἰs ἀλλο γενos,[1] I do not know what Aristotle understood by this designation.[2]

This leads Lessing to the conclusion that ' contingent truths of history can never be made the proof of necessary truths of reason '. This conclusion was important for Kierkegaard in relation to both what he called the argument from the two thousand years and also his point about the subjectivity which the Paradox presupposes.

Now that we have traced some of the important and less important influences which contributed to the development of Kierkegaard's Principle of Subjectivity we shall now see how he states this Principle. We must start from his doctrine of the three stages. It is well known that he distinguished three stages or

[1] Aristotle, *Analytica posteriora*; 7 (75 b). ' It follows that we cannot in demonstrating pass from one genus to another. We cannot, for instance, prove geometrical truths by arithmetic.'
[2] Quoted by Pfleiderer, op. cit., vol. I. pp. 135–6.

spheres of life—the aesthetical, the ethical and the religious.[1] Our concern is with this last stage and its character. Carl Koch has pointed out that as it is described for us in ' Quidam's Diary ', it has five characteristics.[2] The first two are very interesting. First, religion is not a form of doctrine but a way of life. It is a certain way of meeting life's situations of sorrow and joy. Therefore what we have in the Diary is not a scheme of religious thought but a picture of a person living religiously. The second feature arises out of this, and is that religion is a personal matter, something which primarily concerns the individual man. This is seen in the way in which the paramount concern of the young man in the Diary is to answer the question ' Guilty or Not Guilty? ' We can make these two points in another way. The first is that it is wrong to think of religion as being something which consists in making assertions and which has nothing to do with living. The second is that the individual believer is an interested party since the religious life involves him in certain personal problems. Therefore the young man in ' Quidam's Diary ' is not concerned with settling a dispute, but with finding and laying hold of a faith that will give him peace of soul. The important point here is that he himself must find this faith. So when Kierkegaard talks of faith as a personal matter he means that a man does not acquire faith in the same way as he obtains information.

> ' Existential reality is incommunicable, and the subjective thinker finds his reality in his own ethical existence. When reality is apprehended by an outsider it can be understood only as possibility. . . . A communication in the form of possibility compels the recipient to face the problem of existing.'[3]

Kierkegaard is pointing out that when we concern ourselves with proof we are asking the completely wrong question if faith is what we want. When faith asks for proof it sells its birthright for a mess of pottage. Its birthright, its very essence, is the absence of proof. Indeed, religion has no room ' for proof; it is subjectivity '. Ever since 1835 this idea had been very much

---

[1] *Stages on Life's Way*, pp. 188 ff.
[2] Carl Koch, *Søren Kierkegaard*, Copenhagen, 1925, pp. 75 ff.
[3] *Postscript*, p. 320. Cp. *Stages on Life's Way*, pp. 242, 316–17.

in Kierkegaard's mind. For instance, there is the very important
entry in the *Journal* for August 1st, 1835 :

> ' The thing is to find a truth which is true *for me*, to find
> *the idea for which I can live and die*. What would be the use of
> discovering so-called objective truth, of working through all
> the systems of philosophy and being able . . . to show up
> the inconsistencies within each system ; what good would it
> do me to be able to . . . construct *a world in which I do not
> live* but only hold up for the view of others ;—what good
> would it do me to be able to explain the meaning of Chris-
> tianity if it had no *deeper significance for me and for my life*. . . .'[1]

From the close of 1835 Kierkegaard emphasises the need for
subjective appropriation of the truth and regards this as more
important than objective theories.[2] He realises that he cannot
abstract himself though he might abstract from everything else.[3]
Belief is a living relation which in a real sense is a relation with
myself.[4] It is something that is a part of life and there is passion
in it. Even thought is not without its passion—there is a ' breath '
of thought as there is a ' breath ' of air.[5] How can an abstract
knowledge be complete ? he asks.[6] The Hegelian dialectic of
mediate and immediate ultimately leads to nothing.[7]

The first formulation of the Principle in Kierkegaard's work
was the closing sentence of *Either-Or* : ' Only the truth that
edifies is the truth for thee.'[8] This is in effect the problem which
he takes up in the *Philosophical Fragments* where the questions of
learning the truth and the paradoxical nature of truth are discussed. That this is the same theme as that of the end of *Either-Or*
is not evident at once. However, Kierkegaard says in the
Postscript : that the problem of the *Fragments* was not the truth
of Christianity but the individual's relation to Christianity.[9] It
deals with ' the concern of the infinitely interested individual '.[10]
The question is in fact whether learning is the right attitude
towards truth. That it is posed in Socratic language must not
be allowed to confuse our understanding of its point. The

---

[1] *Journals* 22 (I A 75).
[2] Cp. Hirsch, *Kierkegaard Studien*, vol. I, p. 24.
[3] *Papirer*, I A 160. [4] ibid., III A 216. [5] ibid., III A 725.
[6] ibid. III A 160. [7] *Journals*, 72. [8] *Either-Or*, vol. II, p. 294.
[9] *Postscript*, p. 18. [10] ibid., p. 19.

Socratic language is used because it makes the learning of Truth at once a personal matter by its insistence that the truth is in the man. Therefore learning is a relation of the individual to himself. This is inadequate as a description of the way the Christian learns the Truth because it does not recognise the fact that here the Truth is not in man's possession. But once again the important thing is to discover how a man must be related to the Truth in order that it might be his. As for the *Postscript*, it resumes the discussion of this very problem. Once again we have Kierkegaard's own words as evidence of the propriety of our exegesis. In a passage of the *Journal* where he describes the dangers of being a Christian in terms of his new category of subjectivity, he says that becoming a Christian involves the subjectivity of parting with one's understanding and being crucified upon the paradox. And this, he goes on to say, is what the *Concluding Unscientific Postscript* presents in as ideal a manner as possible.[1] So true is it that the religious life is primarily subjectivity, Kierkegaard thinks, that not even the objective creed can escape it altogether; for it begins ' I believe ', and unless this is meaningless it implies subjectivity.[2]

Throughout the *Postscript* this point is reiterated and emphasised and indeed the very problem of the *Postscript* is stated in terms of it. Kierkegaard begins by distinguishing between the objective and subjective ways of dealing with the question of Christianity's truth.[3] He admits the possibility of raising this question objectively but argues that such a method never touches the real heart of the problem. It is only the subjective way of asking the question that can do this because in religion the truth is subjective, and there can be no truth unless it is true for me. So he summarises the objective problem in this way :

' From an objective standpoint Christianity is a *res in facto posita*, whose truth it is proposed to investigate in a purely objective manner, for the accommodating subject is much too objective not to leave himself out, or perhaps he

[1] *Journals*, 843 (IX A 414).
[2] *Journals*, 15.
[3] The words objective and subjective in Kierkegaard correspond roughly to impersonal and personal. Objective is anything that has nothing to do with me. Subjective is what concerns me. The detail of this usage and its implications will become apparent later.

even unhesitatingly counts himself in as one who possesses faith as a matter of course. The truth in the objective sense may mean, first, the historical truth; second, the philosophical truth. Viewed as historical, the truth of Christianity must be determined through a critical examination of the various sources, and so forth; in short, in the same manner that historical truth generally is determined. When the question of the philosophical truth is raised the object is to determine the relationship of the doctrine thus historically given and verified, to the eternal truth. . . . And as for the relationship of the subject to the truth when he comes to know it, the assumption is that if only the truth is brought to light, its appropriation is a relatively unimportant matter ; . . . therein lies the equanimity of the scholar, and the comic thoughtlessness of his parrot-like echo.'[1]

We see even here the double use of the Principle of Subjectivity— the philosophical and the religious. But this need not concern us at the moment. We see that Kierkegaard's point is that neither ' the historical ' nor ' the philosophical ' approach really touches the question with which he is concerned. And since it assumes that this is a small matter, something of no consequence, it is a completely wrong approach. So far from being an unimportant point the relation of the subject to the truth is an essential feature of religion. The historical approach will yield historical results, but it will never produce faith. Faith is always as it were on the horizon and the critical theology always seems about to issue in something relevant to faith. And this is just the difficulty. Suppose we had been able to establish the historicity of the Gospels and all the other things that historical criticism would regard as desiderata. What then? Then the question remains whether we shall acquire faith or not. ' Faith does not result simply from a scientific inquiry ; it does not come directly at all. On the contrary, in this objectivity one tends to lose that infinite personal interestedness which is the condition of faith.'[2] The crux of the matter, then, is this : A historical inquiry aims at producing conclusive evidence, and its assertions are assertions made with reference to the logical coerciveness of these data. Faith, on the

---

[1] *Postscript*, pp. 23–24. [2] ibid., p. 30.

other hand, is an assertion made in passion, and where there is conclusive evidence there can be no passion. Passion gives faith the confidence it needs, and therefore a proof of this sort is not only unnecessary but is actually harmful. ' Faith does not need it ; aye, it must even regard the proof as an enemy.'[1] The same applies to the objective method of speculation. It too makes the mistake of disregarding the person's acceptance of Christianity. As a result it can understand nothing of what really goes on. It will regard Christianity as something merely historical, and so it will endeavour to abstract the essential idea. Thus it tries to make what is in time eternal. This is the speculative philosopher's mistake. The religious subject is ' in passion infinitely interested in his eternal happiness ', but ' to philosophize he must move in precisely the opposite direction '.[2] We see therefore that his ' objective ' way of understanding Christianity is erroneous whether it be objective in the sense of being historical or in that of being speculative. If then the theologian is to describe Christianity he must remember this or else he will do violence to that which he describes. This is the point of saying that it is necessary for the theologian to be ' in subjectivity ' himself. So faith is subjectivity and truth is subjectivity.

It is necessary for us now to analyse what Kierkegaard means by this principle. First, we shall make clear its religious use ; and for this purpose we shall deal with what Theodor Haecker has said about it. Haecker does not discuss this principle at any great length, but he makes a clear and important point. He repudiates—quite rightly—the view that makes the principle synonymous with individualism or subjectivism. Nothing could be further from the truth than this, and the meaning of the principle is precisely the reverse of this. So Haecker calls for a ' theological interpretation ' of its meaning. Understood thus it is part of a syllogism, a syllogism we can state as follows :—

> Since God is infinite subjectivity
> and Subjectivity is truth.
> *Ergo :* God is truth.

This, says Haecker, is the right way to understand this very fruitful thesis that Kierkegaard brought forward.[3] Now even if

[1] ibid., p. 31.
[2] ibid., p. 55.
[3] Theodor Haecker, *Søren Kierkegaard*, Oxford, 1937, pp. 22 f.

this is the way the principle is to be understood the syllogism is wrongly stated because the principle should be the conclusion. That is, the syllogism should be in the Third Figure and not the Fourth, arguing from the premisses that God is Truth and that He is infinite Subjectivity that it follows that Subjectivity is Truth. But is it true that this is the way to understand it ? In the first place, it is extremely doubtful whether this syllogism ever occurred to Kierkegaard. Secondly, and more important, it is true that the principle must be understood in the context of theology, but only in so far as we are talking theology whenever we talk about our religious language. And even then, it does not mean that we have exhausted the meaning of the Principle. For in Chapter II of Part II of the *Postscript*, the principle is discussed in terms of a purely philosophical position.[1] But to return to the original point, let us see what exactly is the religious use of the principle. We can safely say that it is a criterion of faith giving us an essential mark of faith. Kierkegaard insists that only the faith which is characterised by a passionate devotion to its object can be called a true faith. It is this that we must understand by this wonderful parable recounted in the *Postscript* :

> ' If one who lives in the midst of Christianity goes into God's house—the true God's house—with the true idea of God in his mind and prays, but prays in untruth ; and another who lives in a heathen country prays, but with a whole souled passion for infinity, although his eye rests upon an idol ; where then is more truth? The one prays in truth to God though he worships an idol ; the other prays falsely to the true God, and hence worships in fact an idol.'[2]

In a passage in the *Journal* of 1850 Kierkegaard comments that the new situation in Christianity is concerned not with a ' what ' (hvad) but with a ' how ' (hvorledes) ; it concerns in fact a new ' how ' of an old ' what '.[3] This may serve as a commentary on the parable, because he says in an entry just before the one quoted, that it is clear that in his writings he has given a further definition of the concept of faith which thitherto did not exist.[4] Used thus the principle of subjectivity is a polemic against the indifference

---

[1] *Postscript*, p. 169 ff. [2] *Postscript*, pp. 179–180.
[3] *Papirer*, X3 A.593. [4] ibid., X3 A.591.

of the believer who has not realised that if he is a believer he is committed wholeheartedly to his God. The indifference castigated may be either that of saying that a man is a Christian because he lives in a Christian country, or that of saying that faith must be supported by an objective proof.

We may now turn to the philosophical use of the principle. That it is a philosophical principle should be apparent from the fact that its roots were in the German anti-Hegelian movement. As a philosophical principle it is a trenchant criticism of the Hegelian philosophy. It says two things : (1) that no system can do justice to the subtlety of religion because Christian faith by its very nature is inextricably bound up with precisely those things which the system ignores ; (2) that a systematic philosophy (i.e., a metaphysical scheme) is always faced with the danger of becoming either a cliché or indeed a tautology. We shall deal with the second point first as it is in a way easier to handle than the first. And when we look at this closely we see that here again the point is not simple. Let us start by saying that the error of the System for Kierkegaard is that it confuses the fact that one can use the abstract concept ' existence ' with the very different point that it is after all related to empirical assertions. Thus I only speak of existence in terms of things existing. What the metaphysician has been doing, therefore, says Kierkegaard, is trying to make the empirical a matter of logic. Now once he has managed to do this all sorts of things follow. Then—and only then—is it possible for one to construct such a metaphysical scheme as Hegel's in which the real is made identical with thought. But the reason for this is the logical error which we described above. Either then we admit that it is false or we admit that it is a tautology. That is to say, if we continue to maintain that it is real existence or being we are dealing with then we are making this logical error. But the metaphysician may say, 'Ah, now that is exactly where you are wrong, my friend. It is no logical error that I put forward. When I talk of being I am thinking of pure being '.[1] Thus, for instance, Ockham says that metaphysics is the science of being as Aristotle had said, but he also says that

---

[1] Cp. Paul Tillich, *Systematic Theology*, I.17 : ' Nothing can be of ultimate concern for us which does not have the power of threatening and saving our being. The term " being " in this context does not designate existence in time and space.', Cp. p. 22 : ' The suggestion made here is to call philosophy *that cognitive approach to reality in which reality as such is the object*.'

in so far as metaphysics is the science of being as being it is concerned not with a thing but with a concept.[1] Suarez too says that metaphysics has as its proper object being in so far as it is real being.[2] But if this is the case then Kierkegaard's criticism is the general one that the metaphysical assertion of the identity of thought and being is a tautology.

' Whether truth is defined more empirically, as the conformity of thought and being, or more idealistically as the conformity of being with thought, it is, in either case, important carefully to note what is meant by being. And in formulating the answer to this question it is likewise important to take heed lest the knowing spirit be tricked into losing itself in the indeterminate, so that it fantastically becomes a something that no human being ever was or can be, a sort of phantom with which the individual occupies himself upon occasion, but without making it clear to himself . . . what significance being there has for him, and whether the entire activity that goes on there does not resolve itself into a tautology within a recklessly fantastic venture of thought.'[3]

The point which Kierkegaard makes thus is that the systematic philosopher is faced with the dilemma of either making his assertion a matter of ' approximation ' in the sense of trying to do something which can never be finished or making it an absolutely certain matter and thereby making it a tautology. Both alternatives are equally undesirable for him. What he wants is the certainty of the logically certain and empty assertion and the fullness of meaning of the empirical assertion. In other words, he is asking for the impossible.

Another point that is made by means of this slogan is the very important point that in philosophy the reasons for a statement are of greater importance than the statement itself. Lest it be thought that we are reading Twentieth Century Analysis into Kierkegaard's very Hegelian-sounding philosophy, let us remind ourselves of the way he describes results :—

' . . . if inwardness is truth results are only rubbish with which we should not trouble each other. The communication

---

[1] *Ockham, Sentences*, Bk. III 9T.
[2] Suarez, *Disputationes Metaphysicae*. I, 1, 24.   [3] *Postscript*, p. 169.

of results is an unnatural form of intercourse between man and man, inasmuch as every man is a spiritual being for whom truth consists in nothing else than the self-activity of personal appropriation which the communication of a result tends to prevent. . . .'[1]

It need not be pointed out that this constitutes a tremendous blow to the Hegelian philosophy. Dr. Langmead Casserley thus does very well to call Kierkegaard the greatest of Hegel's critics.[2] This is the truth behind Guido De Ruggiero's otherwise very misleading statement that Kierkegaard philosophised in spite of himself. He was no ' médécin malgré lui '. He knew that the Hegelian system had to be attacked and also knew where it needed attacking. In Lessing he found a point of departure for this attack, and it will be instructive to see how the principle of subjectivity is connected with Lessing. After quoting the latter's famous remark that he would stretch out his hand and ask God to give him the search for truth rather than the truth itself, Kierkegaard continues in this ironic vein :

'When Lessing wrote these words the system was presumably not finished ; alas ! and now Lessing is dead. Were he living in these times, now that the System is almost finished, or at least under construction, and will be finished by next Sunday ; believe me, Lessing would have stretched out both his hands to lay hold of it. He would not have had the leisure, nor the manners, nor the exuberance thus in jest as if to play odd and even with God, and in earnest to choose the left hand. But then, the System also has more to offer than God had in both hands ; this very moment it has more, to say nothing of next Sunday, when it is quite certain to be finished.'[3]

The difficulty with the System, thinks Kierkegaard, is that the metaphysician seems to think that he can view things *sub specie aeterni*[4] and thus obtain results which are eternal truths. And

[1] *Postscript*, pp. 216–7.
[2] J. V. Langmead Casserley, *The Christian in Philosophy*, Faber and Faber, London, 1949, p. 150.
[3] *Postscript*, p. 97.
[4] It has been pointed out by Lowrie (*Postscript*, p. 560) that Kierkegaard always uses *specie aeterni* instead of the usual *specie aeternitatis* and that he was far too good a Latinist for this to be accidental. Kierkegaard suggests in fact that the metaphysician is really claiming to be in the same situation as God.

this is precisely what he cannot do because he exists, i.e., is a human being living in space and time. So Haecker says quite rightly that Kierkegaard shifts the emphasis for thought ' from the object to the subject, from the objective world of ideas to the person who has those ideas.'[1] He is right again when he says that ' the being and essence of the person are the elements which Kierkegaard brought into philosophy ',[2] but this needs a good deal of explanation. We shall try to do this by making three assertions which we can then look at more closely. First, it can be said that Kierkegaard brought the person into philosophy in the sense that he will not countenance any philosophy that can be learned by rote. Philosophy must be an activity of an existing person or it is nothing. Secondly, philosophy includes the person for Kierkegaard because the communication of philosophy is an indirect process.[3] It is a fact of some importance that almost all the remarks Kierkegaard makes about Socrates revolve round this point.[4] Finally, the slogan implies that the starting-point and the destination of philosophy are in some sense within the philosopher's own existence. Here Dr. Langmead Casserley is somewhat nearer the mark than he may realise when he places Kierkegaard in what he calls the Augustinian tradition.[5]

To take the first point, Kierkegaard uses the principle of subjectivity polemically against Hegel and against any systematic philosophy by arguing that philosophy cannot be learned by rote. In all probability, had this point been put to Hegel he would have denied that it was his intention to make philosophy something that could be so learned. Yet it was undeniable that his insistence on the value of philosophy as a system of truth resulted in this preoccupation with learning answers. Several years ago R. G. Collingwood said in his *Autobiography* that the primitive thing in philosophy was not proposition but question,[6] and he therefore called for a revision of our statement logic in terms of question and answer.[7] If we hold this point together with Kierkegaard's I think we shall better understand the latter. Philosophy for Kierkegaard was not a matter of making state-

---

[1] Haecker, op. cit., p. 23.   [2] ibid., p. 29.
[3] Vide *Postscript*, p. 68 ff.
[4] Cf. *Journals*, 577, 578, 809, 1376. *Point of View*, pp. 6, 41, 138f.
[5] Casserley, op. cit., pp. 151, 159.
[6] R. G. Collingwood, *Autobiography*, Oxford 1939, pp. 29 ff.   [7] ibid.

ments but rather of a person asking and answering questions in actual existence. Thus he satirizes mercilessly the person who accepts the conclusions of a philosophy without having undergone the process of finding out their truth for himself.[1] The true thinker, according to Kierkegaard, that is, the subjective thinker, chooses not truth but the search for truth. Now Kierkegaard may not have realised, as we do now, that philosophy is not concerned with factual questions and is thus not a search for an answer in the same way as ' Is the light on? ' when we have repaired a fuse. What he did realise, however, was that the important thing in philosophy is the asking of the question. In this sense truth is subjectivity : for the truthfulness of a philosophy is in the way in which it reaches its conclusions. The second point is very closely linked with this and we can see that it follows from it. If philosophy is a person's own activity the communication of philosophy must be accomplished in such a way that it does not result in a ' parrot-like echo '. Kierkegaard felt that Socrates had seen this difficulty and had in his own ' maieutic method ' given an example of how the subjective philosopher works. The important thing is that he does not communicate results.

> ' The reason why several of Plato's dialogues end without results is far more profound than I used to think. It is an expression of Socrates' maieutic art which makes the reader, or the hearer, himself active, and so does not end in a result but a sting. It is an excellent parody of the modern method of learning by rote, which says everything as quickly as possible and all at once, and does not have the effect of making the reader take an active part, but makes him learn it like a parrot.'[2]

To imagine, then, that we can communicate truth directly is to misunderstand the case completely.[3] It was precisely this indirect method that Lessing had revealed—for he too had no results : and Kierkegaard had commended him for that.[4]

The third point is more difficult to handle, and it is not easy to see how Kierkegaard understood this. We shall not be far

[1] *Postscript*, p. 24 et passim.   [2] *Journals*, 578, Cp. ibid., 579.
[3] *Postscript*, p. 223, Cp. ibid., p. 222.   [4] ibid., p. 64.

wrong if we take him to be advocating a philosophy for life. Yet this idea itself bristles with difficulties, the chief of which perhaps is the criticism that philosophy is not a utilitarian science. It is not part of the philosopher's task, we are sometimes told, to provide moral ideas, for instance. This is quite true : but it in no way means that there should be a divorce between philosophy and life. Too often this is admitted because we are dominated by a model of science. But philosophy is not science. Perhaps we shall understand this last point best by returning to a point made earlier, namely that the System is unable to comprehend faith within it and do justice to it because of the subtlety of faith. The System tries to make faith a matter of public assertions. It is like the scientist approaching data and putting them in order and producing the explanation. Faith, on the other hand, is a matter of passionate appropriation and expresses the infinite concern of the person involved. In this way Kierkegaard calls attention to the profound difference between the intimate way in which we *feel* our own trends of thought and action and the cool, detached manner in which we *know* the tendencies of others. I feel the passion with which I pledge myself to the cause of God's Kingdom because the passion is the symptom which reveals its existence. In the case of my neighbour I know that there is like passion in him because I can see certain actions and hear certain utterances. Now Kierkegaard argues that this directness is part and parcel of the way we talk of God. The quarrel he has with Hegel is then that Hegel would try to make God a purely public word. It is not unjust to say that the medieval philosophers were often guilty of the same error. Thus the talk of God as a necessary being, though it was often in such a context as to preclude misinterpretation, did sometimes ignore something essential to the nature of God—that He is the Being whom saints adore and with whom they commune in prayer. To use terminology that Martin Buber has made popular, there is between the believer and God an I-Thou relation which is the very core of faith. To speak of God as the *Ens realissimum perfectissimum* is to gloss over this fact. This is what Kierkegaard means by saying that God is infinite subjectivity and exists only for subjectivity.[1]

[1] *Postscript*, p. 178.

This brings us to the central issue. If it is true that faith is the expression of the individual's concern and that God only exists for subjectivity, does it follow that faith creates its object? In other words, is this principle of subjectivity that Kierkegaard puts forward simply subjectivism? It will not do just to assert, as Dr. Langmead Casserley does,[1] that Kierkegaard's self-consciousness is a consciousness of himself and God. In a way this is true enough; we would certainly agree that this God-ward reference in Kierkegaard's use of ' subjectivity ' distinguishes his thought from that of so many of the ' existentialists '. But it is not quite as simple and straightforward an issue as Dr. Casserley would have us believe when he says :

> ' Kierkegaard thus wins through to a genuine objectivity. . . . Contemporary existentialists, for the most part, have lost this ultimate objectivity and are left with no more than the way of subjectivity through which Kierkegaard approached it.'[2]

The whole point is whether this ultimate objectivity he talks of is objective or not. It is not enough just to say that there is ultimately clear objectivity in Kierkegaard's idea of faith. This is to prejudge the question which epistemology raises. On the other hand, there is a great deal of nonsense talked by responsible people about the anti-rationalism of Kierkegaard so that it is necessary to put in a plea against calling him in an *a priori* way a subjectivist. The evidence to the contrary is the passage where he deals with the truth of Christianity.[3] There he clearly admits the possibility of dealing with the question in an objective fashion ; and his contention is that the ' objective speculative ' approach is not adequate. Moreover, the subjective problem itself is the relation of the individual to the objectively given truth.

We have seen that part of the meaning of the thesis that subjectivity is truth is that in religion every assertion, to be properly understood, must be regarded as having some reference to me. This is what Kierkegaard calls subjective appropriation. But he goes on to make quite clear that this appropriation

---

[1] Casserley, *The Christian in Philosophy*, op. cit., p. 155.
[2] ibid.
[3] *Postscript*, pp. 23-4. Cp. also *Philosophical Fragments* passim where there is ample evidence that Kierkegaard was far from being a subjectivist.

has a certainty which is derived from passion. Since faith is passion its certainty is very different from that of logic or mathematics or again even science. So we are led to the further development of the thesis into the definition of truth as ' objective uncertainty held fast in infinite passion.'[1] Thus Kierkegaard explicitly asserts that for faith to be faith the object must be uncertain. ' Truth is subjectivity ' points to the inconclusiveness or uncertainty of the religious position, to the essential sceptical implication of faith. Elsewhere in the *Postscript* Kierkegaard says that the objective side of the subjective relation appears to us to be a paradox. Thus he says :

> ' Inwardness in an existing subject culminates in passion ; corresponding to passion in the subject the truth becomes a paradox ; and the fact that the truth becomes a paradox is rooted precisely in its having a relationship to an existing subject. Thus the one corresponds to the other. By forgetting that one is an existing subject, passion goes by the board and the truth is no longer a paradox.'[2]

It is not clear from the passage what the paradox is exactly. It would be wrong, however, to identify it with the theme of the Paradox or the Absolute Paradox. For upon careful reading of the passage and the context we see that the paradox is that something uncertain is asserted with passionate certitude as being the truth. Yet Kierkegaard does say in the *Postscript* and in *Training in Christianity* that subjectivity corresponds to the Absolute Paradox—that is, the paradox of the God-Man. For instance, he says :

> ' Christianity has declared itself to be the eternal essential truth which has come into being in time. It has proclaimed itself as the *Paradox*, and it has required of the individual the inwardness of faith in relation to that which stamps itself as an offence to the Jews and a folly to the Greeks—and an absurdity to the understanding. It is impossible more strongly to express the fact that subjectivity is truth and that objectivity is repellence, repellent even by virtue of its absurdity.'[3]

---

[1] *Postscript*, p. 182. [2] ibid., pp. 177–8.
[3] ibid., p. 191. Cp. *Training in Christianity*, pp. 149 ff.

If we examine these two passages that we have just quoted from the *Postscript*, it will become clear that Kierkegaard is really using two ideas of faith when he talks of subjectivity and not only one. Putting the point in another way, Kierkegaard is making two assertions about the use of the word 'faith'. The first is (*a*) that in order that some 'experience' should be called faith its object must not be known in the sense of being demonstrable, since sure knowledge removes the element of risk which is characteristic of faith.[1] The second is (*b*) that since faith is subjectivity then its object, the religious 'truth' is a paradox, and Christianity is the absurd that is asserted in infinite passion.[2] Now it is true that (*a*) does not conflict with (*b*), but it is also true that (*a*) does not imply (*b*). The point that we wish to bring out is that Kierkegaard would want to say both these things. It is perfectly clear that in the *Postscript* and in *Training in Christianity* the paradoxical nature of religious truth is emphasised no less than its inherent uncertainty.[3] We would suggest that (*a*) is the description which Kierkegaard gives of the conditions for using the expression 'faith in God', whereas (*b*) is the description he gives of the conditions for using the expression 'faith in Christ'. This is not a trivial or merely verbal distinction, and we only think that it is because we forget the various uses of the word faith. For instance, in the *Epistle to the Hebrews* we are told that Abraham went out by faith not knowing whither he was going and also that Jesus Christ is the author of our faith. The Old Testament and the New speak of faith in God. The New Testament speaks of the faith of the disciples and the early Church in the Lord Jesus Christ. Thus we say that we know God by faith ; we also say that we have faith in Christ as God Incarnate. We see then that this second assertion is dependent on the first because in the second we are importing a concept into our experience of Jesus Christ, a concept which makes our interpretation of Him a paradox. In this way faith as subjectivity can signify either logical uncertainty merely or a paradox. In both cases, however, there is a contrast between this faith and an assertion that is objectively certain.

---

[1] ibid., p. 182.   [2] ibid., p. 192.
[3] Vide *Postscript*, pp. 186–198, 201–4, 241–2, 514–5, and *Training in Christianity*, pp. 28, 33, 67ff.

Returning to the question of epistemological objectivity we must say quite plainly that Kierkegaard insists that faith requires uncertainty and therefore can never be made a matter of complete objectivity. Indeed, sometimes Kierkegaard uses the word ' subjective ' in such a way that he means something completely uncertain. Such is the correlation between increase in certainty and decrease in religious faith[1] which is very different from the emphasis on the healthiness of passionate trust and adoration in the parable of the pagan and the Christian[2] The danger that confronts us here is that we should complain that Kierkegaard contradicts his essential irrationalism by an attempt to rationalise the paradox. It is most surprising to see such an excellent Kierkegaard scholar as M. Jean Wahl fall victim to this temptation.[3] Then M. Jolivet takes this from M. Wahl lock, stock and barrel. He concludes his book with a chapter in which he discusses ' Kierkegaard's Rationalism.'[4] There he calls Kierkegaard a *Janus bifrons* who, starting with faith and the absurd, constantly tries to ' mediatize ' the paradox and empty it of any significance.[5] And if the paradox is necessary how, asks M. Jolivet, with the blandness of a prosecuting counsel producing the *coup de grace*, can it still be a paradox? To which the answer is, surely, that it is still a paradox because it says two different things at once. Chestov is quoted with approval as saying that Kierkegaard the anti-Hegelian tries hard always to discover dialectical movement, natural development.[6] Dr. E. L. Allen reveals the same inability as Jolivet to appreciate the subtlety of Kierkegaard's talk about the Paradox and he makes the same criticism :

' There is . . . one serious objection to this account . . . Kierkegaard has refuted himself, for does he not labour to remove the offence of which he speaks just by showing that a Paradox which defies reason is only what we ought to expect? '[7]

---

[1] *Postscript*, pp. 182, 189, 192, 204, 453.
[2] ibid., pp. 179–80.
[3] J. Wahl, *Études Kierkegaardiennes*, Paris 1938, p. 434.
[4] R. Jolivet, op. cit., p. 219 ff,
[5] ibid., p. 219.   [2] ibid., p. 219.
[6] ibid., p. 229. Vide also p. 221. The Chestov reference is *Athènes et Jerusalem*, pp. 209 ff.
[7] E. L. Allen, *Søren Kierkegaard, His Life and Thought*, London, 1935, p. 198.

It cannot be too strongly emphasised, then, that the position Kierkegaard enunciates in his slogan ' Truth is Subjectivity ' is not to be identified with an irrationalism. And as we shall see later, he can only be said to ' explain ' the Paradox in so far as he shows that it is the objective aspect of the ' subjectivity ' he describes. But we have admitted that he was quite clear on the question of faith's uncertainty. It cannot be denied that there is a certain exaggeration here as a result of his preoccupation with the risk of faith. He failed to see that the risk is not removed if we can find some reasons, being misled by the false model of scientific reasons. What he means to say is that if there are any reasons for believing, they are not reasons of the kind we have in science. The important point is that here in the religious life reasons will never amount to proof because this life is essentially one of choice and passionate commitment.

We shall now attempt a summary of what Kierkegaard has done by means of this thesis. The first thing he achieved was an extremely powerful criticism of the type of philosophy that he had been taught. This criticism was two-fold. (i) It argued against the view that philosophy could provide results that were definite so that to do philosophy could ever be a matter of assimilating certain information. Philosophy is not a body of facts but the activity of an existing individual. (ii) The attempt to construct a system of general truth to mirror ' Reality ' must always fail—because it can never include the individual person. Then Kierkegaard makes his points about the reduction of religious faith that had taken place in Hegel and his followers. Here he points out that in religion there is nothing that can without violence be made into a logical impersonal statement. That is, any assertion always concerns me. Coupled with this is the emphasis on faith as being a choice. Since it is a choice it is never capable of being transformed into a demonstration. The last general point he makes is that faith is the choice of a way of life or a policy of action. When this is, as in his own case, a Christian faith it is a policy of action based on the assertion of a paradox. Faith is subjectivity and subjectivity is the truth.

CHAPTER IV

THE EXISTENCE OF GOD

The question of God's existence is of the greatest importance in any attempt to consider religion philosophically. From the side of religion and pure (or revealed) theology it is perhaps the first of its dogmatic claims. It is a very difficult question to deal with and one which it is very easy to distort. Indeed the difficulty and the size of the problem make it an acid test of any philosopher of religion. It is no mere hero-worship that makes us claim that no one has written anything on this question which is more significant than what Kierkegaard has written. Let us turn to this question, then, and see how Kierkegaard has helped us to put the question properly and tackle the problem in a fruitful way.

Since the path of faith is that of subjectivity and inwardness we would expect Kierkegaard to correlate the assertion of God's existence with subjectivity. He does this by drawing a distinction between faith's assertion of God's existence and the philosopher's. Thus he writes in his *Journal* :

> ' Immanently (in the fantastic abstract medium of abstraction) God does not *exist*, he only is—God only *exists* for an existing man, i.e., he can only exist *in faith*. . . . Faith is therefore the anticipation of the eternal which holds the factors together, the cleavages of existence. When an existing individual has not got faith God *is* not, neither does God *exist*, although understood from an eternal point of view God is eternally.'[1]

Now it might be said that this remark of Kierkegaard's does not really touch the question of God's existence at all. In a way this is true—and Kierkegaard was quite aware of it. The question of God as posed by this imaginary critic Kierkegaard has called the fantastic abstract being of God. So the criticism is not really very important. Much more important is it to note that, however

[1] *Journals*, 605.

necessary it may be for philosophers to put the problem in this way, for the religious man this is an unreal situation, one in which something vital has been lost. For if this is the case then the existence of God in faith, or to faith, is an aspect of the question which must be brought into our discussion or else our argument will be sterile. It is an interesting and relevant point that those schoolmen, who—more than anyone else—were responsible for the elaboration of the traditional theistic proofs of God, were alive to the importance of this existence (this real existence) of God that Kierkegaard has described. The difficulty was that the very schematism of their work tended to blur their perception of its importance so that the use made of their arguments suggested that this was not an essential feature of the assertion. Thus, when St. Thomas deals with the existence of God in the *Summa Theologica* he says :

> ' The existence of God and other like truths about God which can be known by natural reason are not articles of faith, but are preambles to the articles ; for faith presupposes natural knowledge, even as grace presupposes nature, and perfection supposes something that can be perfected. Nevertheless, there is nothing to prevent a man who cannot grasp its proof, accepting, as a matter of faith, something in itself capable of being known and demonstrated.'[1]

This is very misleading whether we can attribute the misconceptions to St. Thomas or not. It is misleading because it would suggest that the existence of God in faith is not the way this should really be known and is indeed only a second and inferior course. It is like saying to a mentally backward child, ' Now you can take it from me that $2+2 = 4$ '. We can contrast this with the way in which St. Anselm approaches the question. It is quite clear that when he puts forward his ontological argument he is aware of the fact that God really exists only for faith.[2] Thus it is often pointed out that the argument is really a meditation or a prayer. Even so, Anselm assumed that he was giving the ' fool ' a conclusive logical refutation of his assertion that

[1] St. Thomas Aquinas, *Summa Theologica*, Part I, Question II Second Article, Reply Objection I.

[2] Vide *Proslogion* C I & II and É. Gilson's ' Sens et nature de l'argument de St. Anselm ', *Archives de l'histoire doctrinale et littéraire du moyen age*, Paris 1944.

there was no God.[1] It was in fact an attempt to persuade the unbeliever that he had no ground for not believing. We have seen that Kierkegaard has nothing but contempt for proofs. To him proof has no place in religion. The characteristic of faith is subjectivity and not demonstrability. He has a great deal to say about the unsatisfactoriness of the various proofs which we shall now examine in some detail.

In *Philosophical Fragments* he says that whoever attempts to demonstrate the existence of God proves something different, proves indeed, he adds ironically, that he is a man of rare wisdom ! In a note he describes this as ' an excellent subject for a comedy of the higher lunacy.'[2] We shall try to bring out why he regards the attempt to demonstrate God's existence as a ridiculous procedure. The reason is twofold, being partly religious and partly philosophical. It refers back to the fact that God exists only for subjectivity.

> ' The existing individual who chooses to pursue the objective way enters upon the entire approximation-process by which it is proposed to bring God to light objectively. But this is in all eternity impossible because God is a subject, and therefore exists only for subjectivity in inwardness.'[3]

Kierkegaard makes the same point in an extremely subtle analysis of the way in which one loses God when one's prayer becomes a matter of externality.[4] Now, if to believe in God is like this then it is absolutely pointless and indeed downright foolish to assume that we shall produce belief by offering the proof.[5] Connected with this is the comment that ' if God does not exist it would of course be impossible to prove it ; and if he does exist it would be folly to attempt it.'[6] This is a very im-

---

[1] Dr. Mascall points out that the argument itself is ' as purely a matter of the human reason as Euclid's proof of the theorem of Pythagoras '. ' We must not be misled,' he says, ' by the fact that the work in which it occurs, the *Proslogion*, bears the sub-title 'An address to God concerning his Existence ' and has the form of a prayerful meditation, written in the first person and spoken to God himself.' (*Existence and Analogy*, Longmans Green, London, 1949, p. 21.)

[2] *Philosophical Fragments*, p. 34.

[3] *Postscript*, p. 178. Cp. *Journals*, 605.

[4] *Postscript*, p. 145.

[5] Cp. Pascal's remark that a proof will only prove anything to someone who is already convinced.

[6] *Fragments*, p. 31.

portant point and quite different from the first ; and it is one which makes the matter even more foolish. We are now concerned with the *validity* of the argument and not with its success or persuasiveness. The same criticism is made in the *Postscript* when he deals with the ontological argument. He says :

'. . . if God is not really conceived as existing . . . the argument cannot even get started. It would then read about as follows : A supreme being who does not exist must possess all perfection, including that of existence ; ergo a supreme being who does not exist must exist. This would be a strange conclusion. Either the supreme being was non-existent in the premises, and came into existence in the conclusion, which is quite impossible ; or he was existent in the premises, in which case he cannot come into existence in the conclusion.'[1]

The criticism, then, is that the ontological argument presupposes God's existence which is also the conclusion of the argument so that the argument is an instance of the fallacy *petitio principii*. Now it is not very clear how this is so ; for it seems as if the argument's fallaciousness lies in the assumption that existential assertions can be deduced from a definition, and this inclines us to doubt the justice of this charge. Let us attack it in this way. We can point out that a two-value propositional logic does not mean, as Kierkegaard seems to suppose, either that we assert that something is so or deny that it is so. It means, of course, that it is impossible for both ' p ' and ' not-p ' to be true together or at the same time. That is, ' p ' is the negation of ' not-p '. However, this is not saying anything about propositional attitudes ; and there are three such attitudes :—(i) assertion, (ii) denial, (iii) doubt. The logic of this last is difficult, but it is clear that if I assert ' p ' then I am only taking one of three possible attitudes. What we mean can be put in another way. Johnson says in his *Logic*,[2] that there are epistemic conditions (relating to what we *know*) of inference as well as the purely formal condition of implication. Thus Miss Stebbing says that ' the possibility of inference is conditioned by what the thinker

[1] *Postscript*, p. 298.
[2] W. E. Johnson, *Logic*, Pt. I, pp. 2–3.

knows and what is true.'[1] These two kinds of conditions may be stated thus :

Constitutive Conditions.

(i) p must be true : (ii) p must imply q.

Epistemic Conditions.

(i) p must be known to be true : (ii) p must be known to imply q without q being known to be true.

In the special case of the Ontological Argument it appears then that Kierkegaard's criticism does not hold—though he may not be completely wrong. We express ourselves cautiously here, for it will still be true to say that the argument succeeds in drawing the conclusion only as a result of *petitio principii*. The point is that Kierkegaard has grasped the peculiar nature of existential assertions. To prove that anything exists is, he says,[2] a difficult matter. The difficulty is that the proof invariably turns out to be something different from what it is assumed to be, because I will always have assumed that the object exists. ' Thus I always reason from existence and not toward existence ',[3] so that existence is always a datum and can in no circumstances be demonstrated. He shows how this is true by giving two examples—proving that a stone exists and proving the existence of Napoleon.[4] What would it be like to prove the existence of a stone? he asks. The answer is that it would be a demonstration that an existing thing is a stone, and there is more to this answer than meets the eye. For Kierkegaard perceives that the proof cannot bridge the gap between, as he would say, thought and existence, or, as we would now put it, between statements that are *a priori* and those that are *a posteriori*. Consider, for instance, the question of the Abominable Snowman. In January 1954 the *Daily Mail* set out to answer the question ' Does the Abominable Snowman exist? ' How does it answer the question? A photographer is sent out in search of evidence and he reports that he has spoken to people who have seen a strange figure. Now suppose it is not possible to get hold of this figure and bring it back. Suppose that the

---

[1] S. Stebbing, *Modern Introduction to Logic*, p. 214.
[2] *Fragments*, p. 31.
[3] ibid., Cp. *Papirer*, V A 7, 42.   [4] *Fragments*, p. 31.

G

reporter is only able to bring reports of eye-witnesses and photo-graphs. Would not this be a proof of the Snowman's existence? And yet what have we proved? We have proved that the correct description of this figure is to call it the Abominable Snowman. If the reporter were questioned he can be imagined to say : ' This figure looked like this and acted like that. Isn't that what the Snowman is supposed to do? ' We shall see that the same is true in the case of Napoleon's existence, and this is really a closer parallel to God's existence. The attempt to prove the existence of Napoleon from his deeds would, says Kierkegaard, be a most curious process ; for though Napoleon's existence does in a sense explain his deeds, his deeds do not afford a proof of his existence —unless I have already assumed his existence. The way in which I would have assumed this would be in so describing the deeds that the deeds are necessarily simply Napoleon's existence because this is part of their definition. On the other hand, unless I do this the deeds do not prove anything, which means that Napoleon existed. This can be put in another way which would bring out the point very well. What Kierkegaard has done is to show that an attempt to prove the existence of an individual is either an impossibility or a tautology. Thus either all that we manage to prove from the deeds we examine is that the person who was responsible for them was a military genius or else we are able to show that Napoleon was their executor because we have defined them as Napoleon's deeds.

Now it might be thought that the argument for Napoleon's existence fails because there is this element of contingency here : that Napoleon need not have been the author of these actions and they could have been done by someone else. And if this is so, where we fail with Napoleon we are bound to succeed with God, because there can be no contingency here. This is what Kierkegaard calls the ' absolute relationship ' between God and His works. This supposition, however, is of no use.

> ' The works of God are such that only God can perform them. Just so, but where then are the works of God? The works from which I would deduce his existence are not immediately given. . . . From what works then do I propose to derive the proof? From the works as apprehended through

an ideal interpretation, i.e., such as they do not immediately reveal themselves. But in that case it is not from the works that I prove God's existence. I merely develop the ideality I have presupposed, and because of my confidence in this I make so bold as to defy all objections . . .; but what else is this but to presuppose that God exists, so that I really begin by virtue of confidence in him? '[1]

This analysis of Kierkegaard's is extremely important because it lays bare two things : first, the way in which the cosmological arguments must always be fallacious, and secondly, the way in which the religious man always uses the concept of God cosmologically. It is not only to the Psalmist but to every religious man that ' the heavens declare the glory of God and the firmament showeth his handywork.'[2] But just as persistent is the inability of the man who does not believe to see that this is so. What we are trying to say is that this assertion of the relation between the world and God is not a piece of information that can be read off from the appearance of things. It is essential to grasp this point, and if we do we shall see that the cosmological argument does not show the very subtle epistemology of faith as a two-way process. It introduces a concept and deduces the concept once more from the premises. For this reason we do not see that there is much point in saying, as for instance Dr. Austin Farrer does, that ' God must be apprehended in the cosmological relation.'[3] This too tends to make us forget that we are only developing the content of an idea which is a postulate and not a conclusion. The cosmological relation is not something that is clear in the way in which the knowledge of something finite is. It is not clear, for instance, as it is clear to me that my putting a switch on is essentially related to the appearance of

[1] *Fragments*, pp. 32–3.
[2] Psalm XIX.
[3] Farrer, *Finite and Infinite*, London, Dacre Press 1945, p. 45. '. . . there is,' he says, ' no question of demonstrating God from the creatures by a pure inference. God, being a unique existent, must be apprehended if he is to be known at all. But . . . he must be known in the cosmological relation . . . and not in abstraction from it.' This seems harmless enough until we begin to see what this cosmological relation is and it becomes evident that for Dr. Farrer the religious position is an explanation of the finite world. Thus on p. 262 he says, ' We must take some distinction within the finite and then claim to show that the co-existence of the elements distinguished, in the way in which they do exist is only intelligible if God exists as the ground of such a co-existence '.

light. This is very much like Moore's proof of the existence of matter, and we can compare Kierkegaard's comment on the cosmological argument with Wittgenstein's and Wisdom's remarks on Moore's proof. Moore proved that matter existed by lifting first one hand and then another and claiming that it follows from what we know when we say ' Here's one hand and here's another '.[1]   Prof. Wisdom says that ' when Wittgenstein heard Moore's proof of an external world he said : " Those philosophers who have denied the existence of matter have not wished to deny that under my trousers I wear pants ". In fact, Moore's proof is too good to be true—like all good proofs in philosophy its value depends on its invalidity. I must explain myself. To claim that Moore's proof is valid is to claim that " matter exists " is so linked with " I have two hands " that it cannot be more questionable than " I have two hands ". And yet if this is so and " matter exists " is as unquestionable as " I have two hands ", then what is the point of the proof? '.[2]   To repeat Kierkegaard's remark, either God does not exist and there is no valid proof, or God exists and the proof is unnecessary.

The question of God's existence is not, therefore, one which can be settled by a logical demonstration. If this is so, then we must look at the assertion that God exists a little more closely. Prof. Gilbert Ryle has pointed out that most philosophers have followed Kant and paid lip service to the doctrine that ' existence is not quality ' and have rejected the pseudo-implication of the ontological argument that God's perfection entails his existence. ' But,' he continues, ' until fairly recently it was not noticed that if in " God exists " " exists " is not a predicate (save in grammar) then in the same statement " God " cannot be (save in grammar) the subject of predication.'[3]   From this Ryle concludes that the term ' God ' is here therefore a predicative expression. It might surprise contemporary logicians to find this point made by Kierkegaard. In *Philosophical Fragments* he devotes a long note to Spinoza's discussion of God's essence and existence, a note

---

[1] G. E. Moore, ' Proof of an External World ', *Proceedings of the British Academy*, Vol. XXV. 1939, p. 298.

[2] John Wisdom, *Philosophy and Psycho-analysis*, Blackwell, Oxford, 1953, p. 129.

[3] Ryle ' Systematic Ambiguities ', *Logic and Language I* (ed. Flew), Blackwell, Oxford, 1951, p. 15.

which refers to his own remark that ' God is not a name but a concept '.[1] The note is worth quoting :

> ' Spinoza . . . probes the depths of the God-idea in order to bring existence out of it by way of thought, but not, it should be noted, as if existence were an accidental circumstance but rather as if it constituted an essential determination of content. Here lies Spinoza's profundity, but let us examine his reasoning. In *Principia philosophiae cartesianae* pars I, proposotio VII, lemma I, he says : ' *quo res sua natura perfectior est, eo majorem existentiam et magis necessariam involvit ; et contra, quo majus necessariam existentiam res sua natura involvit, eo perfectior.*' The more perfect therefore a thing is the more being it has ; the more being it has, the more perfect it is. This is however a tautology, which becomes still more evident in a note, *nota II* ; . . . *Sed per perfectionem intelligo tantum realitatem sive esse.* He explains *perfectio* by *realitas, esse* ; so that the more perfect a thing is, the more it is ; but its perfection consists in its having more *esse* in itself ; that is to say, the more a thing, the more it is. So much for the tautology, but now further. What is lacking here is a distinction between factual being and ideal being. The terminology which permits us to speak of more or less of being . . . is in itself lacking in clearness, and becomes still more confusing when the above distinction is neglected. . . . In the case of factual existence it is meaningless to speak of more or less of being.'[2]

If we look at Ryle's comments on the ontological argument in the light of this note we see that the issue is not quite as straightforward as he makes out. It will be useful here to look at the

---

[1] *Philosophical Fragments*, p. 32.

[2] *Philosophical Fragments*, p. 32 n. Cp. *Journals* 1027. (*Papirer* X 2 A 328.) 'What confuses the whole doctrine about "being" in logic is that people do not notice that they are always operating with the "concept" existence. But the *concept* existence is an ideality and the difficulty is, of course, whether existence can be reduced to a concept. But existence corresponds to the individual thing, individual, which even Aristotle teaches lies outside or at least cannot be reduced to a concept.' (The reference to Aristotle may be to the polemic against the Platonic Forms which forms one of the leading notes of the *Metaphysica* to which Aristotle returns again and again. There is however in Book I 1, 2, a discussion of how being is applicable to all categories and thus stands above the categories). Cp. also *Papirer* X 2, 36, 48.

ontological argument itself also. The argument is too familiar
to be expounded. This is how Anselm himself stated it :

> ' Convincitur ergo etiam insipiens esse vel in intellectu
> aliquid, quo nihil maius cogitari potest ; quia hoc cum
> audit, intellegit ; et quicquid intellegitur, in intellectu est.
> Et certe id, quo maius cogitari nequit, non potest esse in
> intellectu solo. Si enim vel in solo intellectu est, potest
> cogitari esse et in re : quod maius est. Si ergo id, quo maius
> cogitari non potest, est in intellectu solo, id ipsum, quo
> maius cogitari non potest, est quo maius cogitari potest :
> sed certe hoc esse non potest. Existet ergo procul dubio
> aliquid quo maius cogitari non valet, et in intellectu et in re.'[1]

Now just what is Anselm trying to show? On the face of it it
seems quite unambiguous. Yet scholars disagree very much as
to how the argument should be interpreted.[2] This debate does
not concern us, for our question is a little different. The question
is whether it is true to say that in Anselm's argument ' God ' is
a predicative expression and not a Proper Name. We are prone
to think that Kant demolished Anselm's argument completely,
whereas the truth of the matter is that Kant, like Gaunilo, because
he had seized the fallacy in the argument, failed to see what was
true in it. Anselm expresses a profound insight when he argues
for God's existence from his name. This is that when we speak
of God we are not speaking of something which can be called a
universal.[3] Therefore it is impossible to speak as if there were
certain instances or instantiations which indicate the existence of
this universal. Moreover, we see that it is wrong to imagine, as
Ryle does, that the ontological argument starts with a concept
' aliquid quo nihil maius cogitari potest '. It starts with a Proper
Name which is given this conceptual significance. It does not
follow, then, that if we say that existence is not a predicate then
in ' God exists ' ' God ' is a predicative expression.

It is necessary to bring out this point more clearly if we can.
So let us see what we mean when we say that ' existence is not

[1] Anselm, *Proslogion* c. II, *Sancti Anselmi Cantuarensis Opuscula Philosophico-Theologica Selecta*, Ed. Haas, Tubingen, 1863, I p. 139.

[2] Vide, e.g. Barth, *Fides quaerens intellectum*, and Gilson, op. cit.

[3] It is strange that St. Thomas should make the same point, but it is to be found *expressis verbis* in *Summa Theologica* Part I Question 3, Article 5.

a predicate '. Prof. Moore in his famous essay on this question[1]
says that ' there is some important difference between the usage
of " exist " in "All tame tigers exist " and " Most tame tigers
exist " and the usage of such words as " growl " or " scratch " '.
He compares ' Some tame tigers don't growl ' and ' Some tame
tigers don't exist '. The former has a clear meaning whether it
is tame or not, but the second sentence has no meaning at all if
' exist ' has the same meaning as in ' Some tame tigers exist '.
'A meaning can, of course, be given to " Some tame tigers don't
exist " ; but this can only be done if " exist " is used in a different
way from that in which it is used in " Some tame tigers exist ".
And, if this is so, it will follow that "All tame tigers exist " and
" Most tame tigers exist ", also have no meaning at all." ' Now
that the meaning which ' exist ' has in the sentence ' Some tame
tigers don't exist ' is not the same as the meaning it has in ' Some
tame tigers exist ' might be questioned. But if we said ' Some
tame tigers don't exist ' what would we mean? We would mean
that there are ' imaginary ', ' not real tigers '. And it is clear that
' Some tame tigers do not exist ' is not, then, related to ' Some tame
tigers exist ', in the same simple way in which ' Some tame tigers
do not growl ' is related to ' Some tame tigers growl '. Moore
brings out the second way in which the use of ' growl ' in ' Some
tame tigers growl ' is different from the use of ' exist ' in ' Some
tame tigers exist ' in terms of Russell's analysis of propositions.
' While the first asserts that one value of " x is a tame tiger *and
growls* " is true, the second asserts *not* that more than one " x is
a tame tiger and exists ' is true, but merely that more than one
value of " x is a tame tiger " is true.' ' This is a tame tiger,
and exists ' would be not tautologous, but meaningless. These
two things are what Moore thinks may be part of what is meant
by saying that ' exist ' does not stand for an attribute.

Now the all-important question for us is whether this means
that in the assertion ' God exists ' the term ' God ' is a predicative
expression or not. It can hardly be described as an obvious
implication, and indeed Prof. Ryle's remark becomes much less
persuasive now that the logician's favourite dogma has been
examined. In the first place, when the religious man says that

[1] Moore, ' Is existence a predicate ? ' *Logic and Language II* (ed. Flew) Blackwell,
Oxford, 1953, pp. 82 ff. This section is a restatement of pp. 85 f.

God exists this assertion is not like the assertion ' Some tame tigers exist '. If this latter statement were challenged we should answer that we know of people who have kept tigers as pets, and they were not the least bit ferocious and so on. In other words, the verification of this is to show that there is a value of ' x is a tiger ' such that ' x is tame ' is true. The verification of ' God exists ' can hardly go along these lines because there is nothing we can point at and say ' This is God ' which would be saying that there is a value of ' x is a thing such that x is God ' is true. That is to say, when the fool said in his heart ' There is no God ' this had the same logic as ' Some tame tigers don't exist ' because ' God exists ' is not like ' Some tame tigers exist '. If this is the case then it seems doubtful whether Ryle's claim is true. We can see this even clearer. Let us take three kinds of existential assertions : (i) John exists ; (ii) Mickey Mouse exists ; (iii) Unicorns exist. In both the first and second sentences, the logical subject is the same as the grammatical, and the difference is in the meaning of ' exist '. In the third, however, the logical subject is not ' unicorns '. This is a predicative expression. Now is the assertion ' God exists ' like (i), (ii) or (iii)? It certainly is not like (ii). It might be said to be like (iii), but if this is so, how can we make any sense of the fact that the word ' God ' is used *in the same sense* in ' God exists ' as it is in a prayer such as ' O God unto whom all hearts be open ' and so on? From this we would conclude that it is not possible to classify ' God exists ' as belonging simply to the third class of assertions. The word ' God ' is a Proper Name. Yet is seems equally difficult to put the assertion simply in the first class. A quotation from Dr. Mascall's valuable book *Existence and Analogy* will make this clear. At the very beginning of the first chapter he writes :

> ' The primary task of rational theology is to ask what grounds can be found for asserting the existence of God. Before this inquiry can be profitably initiated, certain preliminaries are, however, necessary. In particular it is essential to be clear . . . precisely what meaning the word " God " is to have in this connection. This is imperative for two reasons. In the first place, the word " God " (and its equivalent in languages other than English) has by no means

always been used in the same sense, and to ignore the difference between the various senses in which it has been used is almost certain to lead us into ambiguity and confusion. In the second place, the word " God " has a very definite meaning in Christian theology, and the rational theologian if he is a Christian, has . . . a very special interest in inquiring into the grounds for asserting the existence of the Christian God rather than that of any of the other beings to which the name " God " has been applied.'[1]

The fact that the first part of this quotation is concerned with the connotation of the word ' God ' while the second indicates that it is used to denote something suggests the complexity of the term. Therefore ' God exists ' is like both (i) and (iii), and Prof. Ryle's criticism does not hold.

In his note on Spinoza Kierkegaard said that Spinoza's profundity lay in just this : that he did not attempt to deduce existence from essence except in so far as he was talking of a conceptual existence. The real difficulty of the problem of God's existence is what we usually mean by existence, that is factual existence. How are we to discover that God actually does exist? We have seen that the attempt to persuade ourselves by means of a proof fails. We do not get to know God's existence in the same way as we can derive the truth of Pythagoras' theorem from Euclid's proof. Indeed the proof if it is used here is only part of the process whereas in the case of the geometrical problem it is the whole of the process of coming to know. How then does God's existence emerge from the proof? Kierkegaard compares it with the behaviour of ' the little Cartesian dolls '. 'As soon as I let go of the doll it stands on its head. As soon as I let it go— I must therefore let it go. So also with the proof for God's existence. As long as I keep my hold on the proof, i.e., continue to demonstrate, the existence does not come out—but when I let the proof go, the existence is there. But this act of letting go is surely also something ; it is indeed a contribution of mine. Must not this also be taken into the account, this little moment, brief as it may,—it need not be long, for it is a *leap*. However brief this moment, if only an instantaneous now this " now "

[1] Mascall, op. cit., p. 1.

must be included in the reckoning.'[1] We come to know God's existence, then, by a leap. Kierkegaard says no more about this in the *Fragments*, but it is an idea that we meet quite often in his other works. It is indeed one of the basic elements in his description of religious knowledge. The connection between this and the principle of subjectivity is clear. The one implies the other. Since religious faith is a matter of subjectivity belief cannot be identified simply with knowledge; and if what we know cannot be proved then it is not knowledge at all.

It is interesting to seek the origin of this idea of ' the leap ' in Kierkegaard. There is no general agreement among scholars on the subject, and the sources suggested by some are indeed very strange. Thus, for instance, Bishop Bohlin would see in this category a recollection of the idea of the qualitative leap which Hegel describes in the *Phenomenology of Mind*.[2] It is difficult to accept this theory because there does not seem to be any parallelism between the two ideas and there is not a shred of evidence that Kierkegaard did in fact borrow the term from Hegel. More plausible is the view Reuter expresses, that the idea is derived from Kant's theory of the jump which takes us beyond experience.[3] This is a much closer parallel, but again it is not sufficiently like Kierkegaard's ' leap '. For one important difference is that this leap that Kierkegaard describes is a particular thing and not a general assertion of something metaphysical. Again, there is no evidence that Kierkegaard was influenced by Kant. Another possible source is Schelling. Now we know that Kierkegaard was influenced by him, and heard him lecture in Berlin. In volume six of the first part of his *Works* Schelling says only by a complete break with the absolute does one arrive at the true and concrete and he calls this a leap.[4] Here again there is no evidence of any direct dependence. It might be thought that we see more evidence of this in the case of the philosopher Kierkegaard did not hear in Berlin, namely Trendelenburg. Of him Kierkegaard said later ' There is no philosopher from whom I have had so much profit as Trendelenburg '.[5] His influence, however, did not lie in the religious use of this term—a fact

[1] *Philosophical Fragments*, pp. 33–4.
[2] Bohlin, op. cit., p. 473. Cp. Hegel, *Werke* II, p. 19.
[3] Reuter, *Kierkegaard's Religionsphilosophie.*
[4] Schelling, *Werke*, I vi. p. 38.   [5] *Journals*, 636.

which we can gather from the dialogue between Socrates and Hegel which Kierkegaard wrote in his *Journal*.[1] In the same way we can disregard the relation between Aristotle's use of the term, which was probably its first appearance in the history of philosophy, and Kierkegaard's category.[2] Indeed, it seems to us that the scholars we have quoted have been strangely neglectful of the evidence in Kierkegaard's own work which points to Jacobi as the source. In the *Postscript* where this idea of the discovery of God's existence by a leap is developed the idea is attributed to Jacobi,[3] and the particular colouring it has in Kierkegaard's use to Lessing. Referring to correspondence between them Kierkegaard says ' Jacobi takes it upon himself to examine Lessing, to find out how things really stand with him. What happens? To his horror he discovers that Lessing is at bottom a Spinozist. The enthusiastic Jacobi ventures upon extreme measures, and proposes to him the only saving *salto mortale* '.[4] Kierkegaard shows how Lessing appreciated the nature of the leap better than Jacobi. Then comes a passage which is extremely important for any discussion of the source of this idea :

> ' For me the little that is found in Lessing has had its significance. I had read *Fear and Trembling* by Johannes de Silentio before I came to read the volume of Lessing quoted above. In that work I had noted how the leap, according to the author's view, becomes as the decision κατ' ἐξοχήν precisely decisive for the Christian categories and for every dogmatic determination. And this is something that cannot be attained either by means of the intellectual intuition

[1] ibid., 552. The entry is entitled ' The Dialectic of Beginning '. Scene in the Underworld. Characters : Socrates, Hegel.' ' Socrates sits by a rippling stream in the cool, listening to the sound of water. Hegel is sitting at a table reading Trendelenburg's *Logische Untersuchungen*, Pt. II, p. 198, and goes across to Socrates to complain. Socrates : Shall we begin by being in complete disagreement or in agreement upon something ?
Hegel : ——
Socrates : With what assumptions do you begin ?
Hegel : From none at all.
Socrates : That is quite possible ; perhaps you do not begin at all."
[2] We might say indeed that it is most likely that the purely logical category of the leap in Kierkegaard derives from Aristotle. He was very familiar with Aristotle's work having had a classical education and also having made a careful study of him later. (Cf. *Papirer* and the auction catalogue of which items 1056–1097 are Aristoteliana.)
[3] *Postscript*, p. 92. Cf. Jacobi, *Werke*, Vol IV, section 1, p. 74.
[4] *Postscript*, p. 92.

of Schelling, or by what Hegel, discussing Schelling's concept with disdain, proposes to substitute for it, namely the Method. For the leap is neither more nor less than the most decisive protest possible against the inverse procedure of the Method. According to *Fear and Trembling* all Christianity is rooted in the paradoxical whether one accepts it as a believer, or rejects it precisely because it is paradoxical. Aye, it lies in fear and trembling, which are the desperate categories of Christianity and of the leap.'[1]

This reference to *Fear and Trembling* might suggest that Kierkegaard was not influenced by Lessing's correspondence with Jacobi in thinking out this idea of the leap. But we know that he had read Jacobi in 1837.[2] The auction catalogue of his library shows that he possessed Jacobi's works and the *Postscript* shows that he was familiar with them.[3] It might be significant that it is only here that Jacobi is referred to in all the *Vaerker*. It is perhaps safe to say, then, that the origin of the term and the idea is in Jacobi. Kierkegaard took it over and sharpened it into the definite concept we have in the *Fragments* and *Postscript*.

The task of understanding what this talk of the leap means is even more difficult than that of finding what historical influences contributed to its formation. M. Jean Wahl says, ' Cette théorie du saut est l'affirmation pour Kierkegaard du discontinu et de l'irrational ',[4] and he goes on to say that one of the ways in which it is used is to describe the nature of belief in God. M. Wahl's description of the leap does not seem to us to be sufficiently clear, and may indeed suggest a quite wrong interpretation of Kierkegaard's philosophical position. It is certainly true that by means of this idea Kierkegaard points to the discontinuity in the process of getting to know God's existence if by this we mean to say that there is no means of demonstrating God's existence or deriving the knowledge of it simply and straightforwardly from an argument. Thus he declares that what carries a man to faith is not the evidence of concepts but the passion of the ideal, the inner conviction.[5] This, however, is a very different thing

---

[1] *Postscript*, p. 96. [2] *Papirer* II A 592.
[3] Items 1722-8 of the catalogue are F. H. Jacobi, *Werke*, 6 Band Leipzig, 1812-25.
[4] Wahl, op. cit., p. 145.
[5] *Papirer* X 2 A 225. Vide ibid. A 354 and X 4 A 365.

from saying, as M. Wahl does in the second part of his sentence, that this signifies irrationalism. Once again we are made aware of the danger of classifying Kierkegaard as an irrationalist. We must guard ourselves against the temptation of dubbing him either ' rationalist ' or ' irrationalist ' and then trying to interpret his complex thought in terms of either category. Does the idea that God's existence is discovered by a leap imply irrationalism? Certainly there are times when Kierkegaard's expressions savour of irrationalism—as for instance when he says that understanding is the death of belief. But even if such passages do express a tendency to irrationalism it is surely true beyond doubt that Kierkegaard never intended to present faith as something quite irrational. Thus Swenson can say ' I have never seen any passage in which Kierkegaard shows scorn for objective validity.'[1]

Having made this clear let us now return to the first point—that the idea of the leap expresses faith's discontinuity. The term is hardly a very happy expression. Not only is the word ugly but it is too easily essentially Hegelian a term for its meaning to be obvious. We shall therefore abandon the term ' discontinuity ' altogether and speak of the incompleteness of the argument for God's existence. Now what does this mean? It means that God can never be the conclusion of any sort of demonstration. The argument for God can proceed quite logically up to a point ; but only by going beyond this do we get our conclusion or affirmation that God exists.[2] The point may be put in another way. One never discovers the existence of God in the way in which one can come to know something about the world which one did not know before. Therefore to imagine that one can speak of knowing God's existence in the way in which one speaks of knowing the existence of dodo birds or again in the way the metaphysician asserts the existence of matter—this is wrong. For both these can be established either factually or logically. The existence of God is discovered by a leap.

It might be thought that since the argument for God's existence is incomplete the religious position is probable rather than certain. So some people think of the religious position as being

---

[1] D. F. Swenson, *Something about Kierkegaard*, Augsburg Publishing House, Minneapolis, Minn., 1941, p. 238.
[2] Cp. *Fear and Trembling*, p. 78 ; '. . . faith begins precisely there where thinking leaves off.'

a hypothesis. Sir Henry Jones, for instance, is reputed to have been fond of saying that the existence of God was the best hypothesis a man could conceive.[1] This is a very dangerous move to make from the point of view of the religious man or theologian, and it is surprising how prone theologians are to think in this way. The model of the calculation of probability is, however, a completely wrong model for describing the logic of the assertion of God's existence. With characteristic irony Kierkegaard paints for us the picture of a man who imagines that faith is a matter of probability.

> ' Suppose a man who wishes to acquire faith ; let the comedy begin. He wishes to have faith, but he wishes also to safeguard himself by means of an objective enquiry and its approximation-process. What happens? With the help of the approximation-process the absurd becomes something different ; it becomes probable, it becomes increasingly probable, it becomes extremely and emphatically probable. Now he is ready to believe it, and he ventures to claim for himself that he does not believe as shoemakers and tailors and simple folk believe, but only after long deliberation. Now he is ready to believe it ; and lo, now it has become precisely impossible to believe it. Anything that is almost probable, or probable, or extremely and emphatically probable is something he can almost know, or as good as know, or extremely and emphatically almost *know*—but it is impossible to believe.'[2]

The probability of the assertion that God exists is not proportionate to the intensity of our faith,[3] and the one thing he fears, Kierkegaard says, is to describe Christianity as being true to a certain degree.[4] It becomes clear, then, that it is neither philosophically nor religiously satisfactory to say that the religious position is probable. So the incomplete argument (M. Wahl's ' discontinuity ') cannot be described as a probable assertion or, rather more precisely, as a probabilifying premiss. If it is not certain that God exists, no more is it probable. This means that

---

[1] Cp. Henry Jones, *A Faith that Enquires*, Macmillan, London, 1922, p. 41.
[2] *Postscript*, p. 189. Cp. ibid., pp. 208-9 et passim.
[3] Cp. ibid., p. 204.   [4] ibid., p. 209

the break in the argument is not an accident : it is an unchange-able situation. We shall not be able to find the assertion that God exists made more probable to-morrow than it is to-day. In other words, the elusiveness of God is due to logical rather than em-pirical reasons.

This brings us back to the matter of hypothesis. We have shown how misleading the model of a probability calculus is. The model of scientific hypothesis is also misleading. There are two respects in which it is misleading. The first point concerns the relation of the evidence to the hypothesis. An important feature of scientific judgments is that once we have a hypothesis to cover the data past and present we put this to the test by trying to make predictions from it. As long as we find the predic-tions confirmed by experience we retain the theory. If, however, the prediction turns out to be wrong then we either modify the theory or abandon it completely. The whole point of having a scientific hypothesis is to have a principle whereby we can make empirical predictions. The usefulness, the value or the validity of the hypothesis depends on the success of the prediction. The existence of God is not at all like this. Thus Kierkegaard says that faith hopes in this life, but by virtue of the absurd.[1] And by the same token he blames himself for the lack of faith that he had shown in breaking with Regina—' Had I had faith I would have stayed with Regina.'[2] Similarly he regards Job's story as showing the high price one pays for faith.[3] Most persuasive of all quotations is this powerful passage on Providence :

' O, the providence of the world is a vast housekeeping, a grandiose painting. Yet he, the Master, God in Heaven, behaves like the cook and the artist. He says : There must be a little pinch of spice here, a little touch of red.—— A little pinch of spice ! That is to say : Here a man must be sacrificed, he is needed to give a particular taste to the rest.—— The birds on the branches, the lilies in the field, the deer in the forest, the fish in the sea, countless hosts of happy men proclaim : God is love. But beneath all these sopranos, supporting them as it were, like the bass part, is the *de profundis* which issues from those who are sacrificed : God is love.'[4]

[1] *Journals*, 445.   [2] ibid., 444.   [3] ibid., 930.   [4] ibid., 1260.

The hypothesis model is misleading in another way too. A hypothesis is always an explanation, a device whereby we explain phenomena and are able to predict like phenomena. If we place a stick in water and notice that it is bent or looks as if it were we can explain this by a scientific theory. The theory is constructed for the purpose of explanation and it is successful only if we are able to predict. That is, the truth of the scientific hypothesis depends upon the repeatability of the phenomena it explains. Now it makes no sense at all to say that God's existence is an *explanation* of anything. That God exists is not a theory put forward to cover any phenomena that have not been otherwise explained. This is partly brought out by Prof. John Wisdom's now famous parable of the garden. Wisdom points out that ' the existence of God is not an experimental issue in the way in which it was ':[1] To show how the existence of God changes from an explanatory hypothesis to something different he relates the following story :

' Two people return to their long neglected garden and find among the weeds a few of the old plants surprisingly vigorous. One says to the other : " It must be that a gardener has been coming and doing something about these plants ". Upon inquiry they find that no neighbour has ever seen anyone at work in their garden. The first man says to the other, " He must have worked while people slept ". The other says : " No, someone would have heard him and besides, anybody who cared about the plants would have kept down these weeds ". The first man says : " Look at the way these are arranged. There is purpose and a feeling for beauty here. I believe that someone comes, someone invisible to mortal eyes. I believe that the more carefully we look the more we shall find confirmation of this ". They examine the garden ever so carefully . . . they also study what happens to gardens left without attention. Each learns all the other learns about this and about the garden. Consequently, when after all this, one says " I still believe a gardener comes " while the other says " I don't " their different words now reflect no difference as to what they would find in the garden if they looked further and no difference about how

[1] Wisdom, *Philosophy and Psycho-analysis*, Blackwell, Oxford, 1953, p. 149.

fast untended gardens fall into disorder. At this stage, in this context, the gardener hypothesis has ceased to be experimental.'[1]

The difference between the person who asserts the existence of the gardener and the one who denies it, says Wisdom, is in the way they feel towards the garden. We have quoted Wisdom's story fully because it shows two things—(1) that we are right in saying that God is not an explanation ; (2) that we are prone to regard the assertion that God exists as being an explanatory hypothesis. It is a weakness of Wisdom's discussion that it should assume that the belief in God should at any point in religious language be capable of being regarded as an explanatory hypothesis. He seems in fact to suggest that only when it has been shown not to succeed as such that the belief attains its peculiar character. Kierkegaard's contention, on the other hand, is that even in the case of the cosmological argument, where it is nearest to being an explanation, the belief is not reached by means of explanatory argument but in fact by a leap which means that we no longer *explain*. If we imagine that the existence of God is something derivable from certain evidence then we are making it the fantastic thing that Kierkegaard said the philosophers had made it. This is to move in the abstract medium of thought and to miss the most important feature of belief in God. Here we have the essential difference between religious faith and any faith that may be claimed to lie behind the scientist's method. The first is the choice of a policy of action which is bound up with a metaphysical concept and indicates part of that concept's meaning. We have now come back to the point where we began —the existence of God to faith. We can only talk of God's existence as being what is known in subjectivity.

There is another point that Kierkegaard makes in his use of this idea of the leap. It is this : to say that God exists involves a risk.[2] Now, it is true to say that there is risk here because it is a synthetic statement and not an analytic one ; but this is trivial. The risk is much greater than that of knowing but perhaps I am mistaken though I don't now see how I can be. It is the risk of saying ' I know my Redeemer liveth ' when no evidence

[1] ibid., pp. 154–5.   [2] *Postscript*, pp. 182, 188.

can be seen that makes it credible. It seems to us that Dr. Croxall does not quite appreciate the force of this point when he imagines the leap as that made by one of a party of mountain climbers. ' When we need to leap a crevasse on an ice-bound mountain, it is better, safer, and gives more confidence if we are roped to others, and gives us courage.'[1] The picture this gives us is quite other than what Kierkegaard suggests by his emphatic remarks about the leap, describing it as the absolute leap, the *salto mortale*. The picture Croxall gives is not that of walking in the shadow of death, of tremendous venture. If we fall the others will haul us up and we need not be afraid. But there is no guarantee of safety for faith. No one can help us—we have to fend for ourselves. When we draw ourselves together for that great leap we do so because we are prepared to risk falling into the crevasse. With our life in both hands we—leap. This is a clear expression of the hazard of religious thinking.[2] I cannot know before I leap that there will be life the other side of the crevasse. Indeed even after the leap the only certainty I have is that which carried me over. Kierkegaard describes this in a characteristically graphic way :

> ' Sitting quietly in a ship while the weather is calm is not a picture of faith ; but when the ship has sprung a leak, enthusiastically to keep the ship afloat by pumping while yet not seeking harbour : this is the picture. . . . While the understanding, like a despairing passenger, stretches out its arms towards the shore, but in vain, faith works with all its energy in the depths of the soul : glad and victorious it saves the soul against the understanding.'[3]

The choice or the leap is made in passion. It is not a matter on which we can build up a degree of assurance that we have here. If we are going to be sure we have to leap. And conversely we are sure, passionately sure only when we have taken the leap. Belief in God is ' the highest passion of subjectivity, of the inwardness of subjectivity, the passion of passion.'[4] In his *Journal* Kierkegaard describes the certainty of faith as *a priori* :

'As there is an *a priori* certainty by comparison with

[1] T. H. Croxall, *Kierkegaard Studies*, Lutterworth Press, London, 1948, p. 75.
[2] *Postscript*, pp. 182, 380–1.   [3] ibid., p. 202 n.
[4] Cp. VI, pp. 110, 132, 212, 284.

which all empirical fact is evanescent so faith is the *a priori* assurance before which all the empiricism of action disappears.'[1]

This certainty of faith he later described as ' the second immediacy '[2] or ' the immediacy after reflection '.[3] It is very difficult to make clear what is involved here because he has insisted that faith is not to be confused with any immediate cognition or indeed any sort of cognition.[4] Nothing could be more definite on this point than this entry in the *Journal* of 1853 : ' Consequently we . . . have no immediate relation to God.'[5] We might with a great deal of justice interpret Kierkegaard's whole output as a protest against the identification of faith with immediacy. To make clear what is involved in this distinction between the first and the second immediacy we must try to understand what Kierkegaard means by immediacy in the different contexts. This passage from the sermon for the feast of Pentecost published in 1851 throws some light on the question :

' (The Spirit) brings *faith*, ' faith ', that only being in the strictest sense faith which is the gift of the Holy Spirit after death has come between. For we men are not so precise in the use of words, we often speak of faith when in the strictest sense it is not faith. In every man with differences due to natural endowment, a stronger or weaker spontaneity (immediacy) is inborn. The stronger, the more vitally powerful it is, the longer it can hold out against opposition . . . when all confidence in thyself or in human support or in God as an immediate apprehension, when every probability is excluded . . . then comes the life-giving Spirit and brings faith.'[6]

This, however, gives only part of the way towards clarifying the term for us ; and if we are to understand it fully we must look to Hegel from whom Kierkegaard obtained the term. In Chapter V of the *Logic* Hegel discusses the attitude of Jacobi and his like to objectivity under the title ' Immediate or Intuitive Knowledge '. He describes the intuitional theory as holding that thought is ' an act of the *particular* only, and on that ground

[1] *Papirer* I A 316.   [2] *Fear and Trembling*, p. 125.
[3] *Papirer* VII A 650.   [4] *Journals*, 10, 78, 753.
[5] ibid., 1289 Cp. *Postscript*, p. 218.   [6] *For Self-Examination*, pp. 100-1.

declares it incapable of apprehending the Truth '.[1] Thinking, on this view, is a private operation using the categories which are limited vehicles of thought and which cannot comprehend the infinite and unconditioned without perverting the truth into untruth. This is the essential argument put forward for the position that the knowledge of God must be immediate or intuitive. The clearest exposition of this type of argument, says Hegel, is to be found in Jacobi's seventh supplement to his letters on Spinoza where Jacobi borrows his line of argument from Spinoza and applies it as a weapon against knowledge in general. ' In his attack knowledge is taken to mean knowledge of the finite only, a process of thought from one condition in a series to another, each of which is at once conditioning and conditioned. According to such a view, to explain and to get the notion of anything, is the same as to show it to be derived from something else. Whatever such knowledge embraces, consequently, is partial, dependent and finite, while the infinite or true, i.e., God, lies outside of the mechanical inter-connexion to which knowledge is said to be confined.'[2] At the same time Jacobi declares that man lives by Reason alone. This Reason is the knowledge of God, a knowledge which, because of its underivative character, is called Faith. ' This immediate knowledge consists in knowing that the Infinite, the Eternal, the God which is in our idea, really is.'[3]

We can now see what Kierkegaard was denying. Faith could not be said to be immediacy because it was not some peculiar feeling that was destroyed by intellection.[4] Further, as Hegel himself had pointed out in connection with Jacobi,[5] this philosophical faith is sufficiently vague to describe anything. Kierkegaard takes this point further and argues that inasmuch as Hegel too and his followers with him imagined faith to be something immediate they were confusing for faith what was nothing more than the condition of all thinking.[6] There is another thing that

---

[1] *The Logic of Hegel* (trans. Wallace), Oxford 1892, p. 121.
[2] op. cit., p. 122.   [3] ibid., p. 126.
[4] Cp. *Postscript*, p. 310.   [5] op. cit., p. 125.
[6] The reference is to *Papirer* I A 273. For Hegel vide op. cit. p. 52. In this entry to the *Journal* Kierkegaard speaks of Hegelian dogmatists and is probably thinking of Marheneike. The latter's *Die Grundlehren der Christliche Dogmatik als Wissenschaft*, p. 6 could be the reference he has intended because *Papirer* I C 25. is a translation of pp. 4–10 of this book.

Kierkegaard may be presumed to be attacking by his denial that faith is immediacy. This is the indubitability of what is immediately known. If I know anything immediately I cannot doubt it. Indeed to say that something might be doubted but that we know it immediately is a very peculiar kind of statement. The peculiarity arises from the fact that what we know immediately is our own feelings. Thus we would say that I know immediately that I have a headache, but I do not know immediately that my friend has a headache. Immediate knowledge is therefore a matter of autobiographical assertions. Kierkegaard saw that the idea which dominated theology and religious philosophy in his time made faith safe at the cost of transforming it into something it was not, and reducing it in fact to nothing more than feeling. He saw that this was the undesirable consequence both of Schleiermacher's definition of religion as a feeling of absolute dependence and of the Hegelian description of faith as immediate knowledge. To avoid this error he put forward his assertion that faith is not immediacy. That is, ' God exists ' can never be equivalent to ' I feel God's existence ' where ' feel ' is used in the same way as it is in ' I feel that I have a headache '.

Now what does all this mean? It means that ' God exists ' is as dubitable a proposition as ever it was. It is not less dubitable when we have made the leap than it was before. Does this mean that the leap achieved nothing? Not at all : the leap has achieved everything. Now we believe : before we did not. One thing we know—whereas before we were blind now we can see. It is just this which makes Kierkegaard throw consistency to the winds and reintroduce the concept of immediacy. Thus he says of the Hegelian philosophy that ' it is not warranted in regarding Abraham as the father of faith and in talking about faith. For faith is not the first immediacy but a subsequent immediacy. The first immediacy is the aesthetical, and about this the Hegelian philosophy may be in the right. But faith is not the aesthetical— or else faith has never existed because it has always existed '.[1] In two consecutive entries to the *Journal* of 1848 he discusses the theme of faith as the second immediacy.[2] Here it appears that by this he means that faith only comes into being when a simple conviction expressing hopeful feelings has been left be-

---

[1] *Fear and Trembling*, p. 125.   [2] *Journals*, 753, 754.

hind. Then it is seen for what it really is—the assertion of God in the face of all the evidence which seems to make nonsense of saying that He exists. Now the all-important point here is that there is, as Kierkegaard says, a certainty in this assertion which is quite incommensurable with the evidence. So we see once again how foolish it is to think of faith in terms of probability. There is one sentence in the *Postscript* which illuminates this difficult idea very well. It speaks of faith as ' the new immediacy . . . which can never be abrogated in existence since it is the highest immediacy '.[1] That is to say, though faith cannot be spoken of simply in terms of immediate awareness as a great number of philosophers and theologians have tended to do in recent years, yet it shares with such awareness the character of being able to say without evidence ' I know God exists '. And to ask ' How do you know that He exists? ' is answered only by Abraham's silently taking Isaac to Mount Moriah.

[1] *Postscript*, p. 310 n.

CHAPTER V

THE ABSOLUTE PARADOX

For Kierkegaard the object of faith must by definition be something uncertain—that is, objectively uncertain. This contrasting certitude (inner certainty) and uncertainty (objective lack of certainty) of faith he called the paradox of faith.[1] This is the paradox that we have discussed in the last two chapters. It is necessary, however, to distinguish two main uses of the word ' paradox ' in Kierkegaard's language. The first is that use which describes the contrast between the logical evaluation of faith and its psychological character. This use we may call the broad use to distinguish it from the other use which we may call the narrow use. This narrow use of the word is the description Kierkegaard gives of the specifically Christian faith and the object of such faith. Thus he says very often that Christianity is the Absolute Paradox and also that Christian faith is faith in the Absolute Paradox, the God-Man. This Paradox is the special stumbling-block of Christianity.[2] It is true that this peculiarly Christian faith is compatible with the general characterisation of religious faith as paradoxical. However, what Kierkegaard means by this idea of the Absolute Paradox has little to do with what we have called the broad use of the word. Dr. J. V. Langmead Casserley does not seem to be aware of the two different meanings of the word Paradox in Kierkegaard. Thus he argues that Kierkegaard wrongly assumes that the way of paradox is peculiar to our apprehension of God. In fact, he continues, this is the difference between Kierkegaard's way of paradox and his own—that he recognises that the apprehension of the unique always involves paradox.[3] This is to miss completely the point that Kierkegaard distinguished the central Christian concept from all other paradoxes for the simple reason that it is quite different from them. Kierkegaard was quite aware of the importance of paradox for any knowledge of any human situation as is seen from the way he describes ' the paradox of the forgiveness of sins ',[4] and again the remark in the *Journals* that ' paradox is really the pathos of

---

[1] *Postscript*, pp. 183. Cp. pp. 180–6, 187.   [2] ibid., pp. 194–5.
[3] Casserley, op. cit., p. 182.   [4] *Postscript*, pp. 201 f.

intellectual life—and . . . paradoxes . . . are only grandiose thoughts in embryo '.[1] There is mention of paradox in *Fear and Trembling*[2] which is probably the first time Kierkegaard interpreted faith as paradox. But it was in *Philosophical Fragments* that he first broached the question of the Absolute Paradox[3]—and this is our concern.

Before we proceed to an exposition and examination of this theme we shall try to discover its historical sources. What are the influences which led Kierkegaard to this position? His use of the category of paradox in the broader sense as the category for all religious assertions can safely be said to derive from Hamann. One reason would be that this theme of paradox is but the other side of the theme of subjectivity and an important source of the latter is the irrationalism of Hamann.[4] So it could be said that there is a prima facie case for the view that Hamann is one of the sources of this theme. This can be supported by looking at the development of the idea of paradox in Kierkegaard. We have seen how important a discovery for him was his discovery of Hamann's championship of the paradox of faith's certitude and uncertainty. In an early volume of the *Journal* he describes how impressed he was by the fact that after reading one of Hume's most powerful objections to Christianity Hamann was not in the least disturbed but remarked quietly, ' Yes, that's exactly how it is! '[5] This he copies in his remark in the *Journal* ' Incredibile sed verum! Lies . . . must be plausible . . . but not the great truths . . . of our faith.'[6] Years later he associates his assertion of the incomprehensibility of faith with Hamann.[7] All this gives us ample evidence of Hamann's influence. And the discussion of the Paradox in the *Fragments* directly refers to him as the source of the remarks made.[8] Our problem is, however, far from settled ; for if Hamann is mentioned so too is Tertullian. Once more the imaginary critic points to the source of Kierkegaard's remark saying that the quia absurdum is derived from Tertullian.

[1] *Journals*, 206.
[2] *Fear and Trembling*, p. 52. Cp. pp. 56 and 57.
[3] *Fragments*, p. 29ff.
[4] Cp. Lowrie, op. cit., p. 164 and also his *Hamann an Existentialist*, Princeton,1951.
[5] *Papier* I A 100. The reference is to Hamann *Werke* I p. 406. Cp. pp. 418, 419, 443.
[6] *Papirer* I A 237.
[7] ibid., X 2 A 225.   [8] *Fragments*, pp. 42-3.

Kierkegaard may have in mind the aphorism ' credo quia absurdum ' which is usually attributed to Tertullian but is not to be found in his work. However, it is a useful enough way of characterising Tertullian's interpretation of the Christian faith.[1] A most telling entry in the *Journal* strengthens the supposition that we have evidence of Tertullian's influence in the idea of Paradox. It is this :

> ' *Christianity—Tertullian.*
>
> I have often said that Christianity can be represented in two ways : either in the interest of man (an extenuating adjustment), or in the interest of God (true Christianity). I have also said that if I do not succeed or dare to present Christianity in the latter form I shall admit it and keep the place free.
>
> Hardly any of the early Fathers present Christianity in God's favour with the same emphasis as Tertullian. . . .'[2]

We discover from the *Journal* that in 1839 Kierkegaard had been reading about Tertullian's theology,[3] and later in the same *Journal* he says that he can ' still find rest in the shade of the noble alley of the Fathers '.[4] Again, the theory could still be maintained even were it proved that Kierkegaard did not arrive at this position as a result of reading Tertullian in 1839. For in 1842 he was reading Leibniz's *Théodicée*[5] and in the introduction Leibniz quotes a remark of Tertullian in *De Carne Christi*. It is, therefore, almost impossible to doubt that Tertullian did influence Kierkegaard at this point—whether directly or indirectly we need not ask now.

The matter begins to have an appearance of clarity, but again a whole crop of difficulties arise. Reuter argues that ' Kierkegaard's ideas about religious philosophy have received their form and character from the Hegelian treatment of these problems ' and in particular that the idea of Paradox has its origins in Hegel's

---

[1] Cp. *De Carne Christi* c.V. ' Mortuus est Dei filius, credibile est quia ineptum est ; et sepultus revixit, quia impossibile.'   [2] *Journals*, 1192.
[3] *Papirer* II A 446.
[4] ibid. II A 750. (Dru 203) This should read : ' Still, however, sometimes find repose.'
[5] *Papirer* IV C 29. The *Théodicée* is item 619 of the Library catalogue of which item 622 is a book on Leibniz as a theologian by C. Schwarz (Halle 1854). The works of Tertullian are also included—items 147-50.

theory of contradictories.[1] This is to fly in the face of all the
evidence and can hardly be given any credence. Niels Teisen
has contended that the concept is derived from traditional
Christian theology. He argues that Kierkegaard accepted the
orthodox faith without criticism and so he came to rely for his
essential theology on Augustine and Athanasius.[2] The difficulty
with Teisen's view that Kierkegaard's doctrines of the paradox
and of sin were due to Athanasius and Augustine respectively
is that it was not apparently reached by any historical criticism.
It is not even based on those entries in the *Journal* and other
parts of the *Papirer* where Kierkegaard openly accepts the views
of the Church Fathers. How Teisen came to hold this view is
not at all clear from his treatise. Probably the mention of the
word 'Paradox' as a description of Christ and the radical interpretation of sin instantly put him in mind of the Athanasian
Christology and the Augustinian doctrine of original sin, an
association of ideas which would be natural enough for a theologian. It is rather strange that, though Bohlin gives a fuller treatment of this point than does Teisen, he too fails to give any
other grounds for his assertion that Kierkegaard is dependent
on these early theologians than the striking agreement between
his and their views.[3] Drachmann, one of the editors of Kierkegaard's works, has shown, however, that this is not the only
possible explanation of the source of these ideas. In a lecture
entitled 'Paganism and Christianity in Søren Kierkegaard' he
put forward and substantiated the view that it was his relation to
Socrates, 'the Socratic', that was decisive for Kierkegaard's
moulding of his belief.[4] Drachmann maintains that the Christian
definitions in *Philosophical Fragments* (the Paradox and Sin) were
not developed from Christianity itself but that Christianity is
there built up constructively as a contrast to the humanistic view
of life which Socrates represents in the history of the world.
This, it is supposed, is the reason why the dogmas of Christianity
such as the Trinity, the Holy Ghost, are not included in Kierke-

---

[1] Reuter, op. cit., p. 124. We saw that Reuter tries to derive the leap from
Hegel too. This is to say then that all of Kierkegaard is in Hegel !
[2] Niels Teisen, *Om Søren Kierkegaard's Betydning som Kristelige Taenker*, Copenhagen, 1903, p. 41.
[3] Bohlin, op. cit., pp. 216, 432.
[4] Drachmann, *Udvalgte Afhandningler*, 1911, pp. 124 ff.

gaard's teaching. His point of departure is the Socratic one that viewed absolutely all men are equal, there being only one distinction in the absolute, namely that between man and God. Man can learn the most important things of existence only from God and not from another man. If, therefore, a man is to accept the teaching of Christ, as Christianity demands, then it must be that Christ is God. At the same time however He is a particular person who lived at a definite time, and can be recognised as a historical figure. To say both these things is to say that He is the Paradox. Drachmann's point is that in order to maintain the Socratic idea of the equality of men within the context of Christianity Kierkegaard had to discount the doctrine communicated by tradition and make everything depend on the fact that the teacher was God. This argument is an extremely ingenious and interesting argument. Because he is able to make out a case for it Drachmann's argument makes a very powerful criticism of Bohlin and Teisen. The argument is, however, too ingenious on the one hand and too naive on the other. Its naivete lies in the way in which it seems to regard Kierkegaard's Christianity as quite devoid of content. Moreover, it does not at all explain something which can be explained easily on the other view, namely how Kierkegaard came to hold that there is an absolute difference between God and man. And if Drachmann's argument is to be sustained it must be explained how Christ's doctrine was all-important for Kierkegaard apart from the incarnational theology. In each case here it is much easier to say that Kierkegaard approached Socrates with a definite background of Christian thinking and that the theme of Paradox springs from this thinking. These considerations lead us back to Bohlin's and Teisen's view which now appears to have more truth than evidence on its side. Himmelstrup has, however, made a very valuable suggestion which is something of a compromise between these two views.[1] He says that the assumption of the absolute difference between God and man may derive from Socrates, to whom at any rate Kierkegaard ascribes the distinction. But he also says that it may equally well derive from the Athanasian doctrine of the dual nature. This means that Drachmann's argument is essentially one-sided and his problem could only be solved by taking into

[1] J. Himmelstrup, *Søren Kierkegaards Opfattelse af Sokrates*, p. 247.

account the fact that the Athanasian doctrine is itself a product of Greek thinking.[1]

The conclusion to which we are led, then, is that the idea of Paradox as used in the sense of the Absolute Paradox is derived from both Tertullian and Athanasius and receives its form in the *Fragments* in the context of the discussion of Socrates. It is as well to indicate here the evidence for saying that Athanasius did influence Kierkegaard. The first point is that he obviously must have acquired some knowledge and understanding of Athanasius during his theological studies. A volume of patristic writings is found amongst his books, but was published too late to be relevant to this discussion.[2] However, there were three books that are relevant. They are : Hase's *Libri Symbolici*, Möhler's two volume work on Athanasius, and Görres' *Athanasius*. On April 15th, 1839, Kierkegaard wrote in his *Journal*, ' I have read the *Athanasius* of Görres not only with my eyes but with my whole body. I have read it with my entrails '.[3] (We know from the *Papirer* that he read Möhler's work with great care). We have already quoted his remark about finding solace in the Fathers.[4] We are surely perfectly justified then in saying with Geismar that there is no doubt that Kierkegaard presents the Christian faith in the person of Jesus Christ as true man and true God in perfect conformity with the Athanasian creed.[5]

So much for the question of the origin of his idea of the Absolute Paradox. Let us now see what Kierkegaard actually says about this. Chapter II of the *Fragments* 'A metaphysical crotchet ', deals with the Absolute Paradox. He begins by telling us that ' the paradox is the source of the thinker's passion, and that the thinker without a paradox is like a lover without feeling, a paltry mediocrity '.[6] That we are wrestling with a paradox is a sure mark of the value of our thinking. But since this thinking contains passion it will end in thought destroying itself. This is

---

[1] Cp. Harnack, *History of Dogma*, vol. I, pp. 48–9, 56n. 2.
[2] *Patrum apostolicorum opera* (ed. Hefell) Tübingen, 1847, (catalogue No. 152).
[3] *Papirer* II A 728. Görres' book was published in 1838. Hase's *Libri Symbolici* in 1837 in Leipzig, and Möhler's work in 1827. They are Nos. 1073, 624, and 635 of the catalogue.
[4] *Journals* 203, Cp. *Papirer* II C 30 for Möhler's *Athanasius*.
[5] E. Geismar, *Lectures on the Religious Thought of Søren Kierkegaard*, Augsburg Publishing House, Minneapolis, 1937, p. 63.
[6] *Fragments*, p. 29.

the paradoxical passion of Reason, that it should seek collision with something when this collision will prove its undoing. Kierkegaard illustrates this by showing the analogy between this and the paradox of love.[1] This something the Reason collides with is the ' Unknown ', which we may call God. It is folly to attempt to prove God : for, as we have seen, he points out that this would assume the existence of God at the outset. Argument moves from and not toward existence. So Socrates would never have dreamed of proving the existence of God.[2] He is indeed credited with having propounded the physico-teleological proof, but he did not start without assuming God's existence. ' He always presupposes God's existence, and under this presupposition seeks to interpenetrate nature with the idea of purpose.'[3] Reason is thus forever coming into collision with the unknown. This is the limit of Reason's reach ; it cannot go further than this, but yet it comes to it again and again. To say that it does not exist is just nonsense because this in itself expresses the limiting concept. What then is the Unknown? It is ' the limit, the different, the absolutely different '.[4] From this it follows that if Reason is to know anything about this Unknown it must know that it is the different. This raises the difficulty of how Reason can know the different. ' When qualified as absolutely different it seems on the verge of disclosure, but this is not the case ; for the Reason cannot conceive an absolute unlikeness.'[5] Reason can have this knowledge then only as it obtains it from God. The unlikeness is sin. Socrates was perplexed, says Kierkegaard, because he lacked a consciousness of sin, which he could only learn from God. ' In order to be man's Teacher, God proposed to make himself like the individual man so that he might understand him fully. Thus our paradox is rendered still more appalling, or the same paradox has the double aspect which proclaims it as the Absolute Paradox ; negatively by revealing the absolute unlikeness of sin, positively by proposing to do away with the absolute unlikeness in absolute likeness.'[6] The paradox may or may not be accepted. If it is not, the person who rejects it is ' offended '. Kierkegaard makes great use of this category of ' offence ', particularly in *Training in Christianity*. Here he points out that it expresses a

[1] ibid., p. 30.   [2] ibid., p. 34.   [3] ibid.
[4] ibid., p. 35.   [5] ibid.   [6] ibid., p. 37.

passive state, thereby indicating that our very rejection of this is made on the basis of knowledge derived from the Paradox.'[1]

> ' But precisely because offence is thus passive, the discovery, if it be allowable to speak thus, does not derive from the Reason, but from the Paradox. . . . Offence was not discovered by the Reason, far from it, for then the Reason must also have been able to discover the Paradox.'[2]

Offence rejects the Paradox *quia absurdum*, but the Paradox is the Paradox *quia absurdum*.'[3]

A problem of interpretation arises here which it is as well to discuss before we move on to a further exposition of the idea of the Paradox. Scholars disagree on the question of how to understand this term as it is used here in the *Fragments*. We have already met the idea that the Paradox is essentially a Socratic concept—this was Drachmann's argument. There is a similar point made by Theodor Haecker who also thinks that it is an artificial construction. Haecker maintains that in the *Fragments* God is ' not the historical Jesus Christ of the seed of David, who was foretold and came amid signs and wonders ; he is a poetic creation, the aim of which is to stress the paradox that a man is God—by exaggerating it '.[4] In this the majority of scholars would probably not agree with Haecker. Certainly both E. L. Allen and H. R. Mackintosh can be quoted against him.[5] It seems to us that these scholars' view is sounder than Haecker's for the reasons which we have already mentioned in our discussion of Drachmann's theory. Surely the Paradox is the term Kierkegaard used to describe the Word becoming flesh which is so far from being artificial that the Fourth Gospel states it as a historical fact. And by using this term in the *Fragments* and *Postscript* Kierkegaard called the attention of his contemporaries to an aspect of the Christian dogma that was vital and had been clouded over by the work of the Hegelian theologians. This line of thought concentrated on the paradox of asserting that a historical figure was God. The significance of the *Fragments* in this respect does not appear clearly until it is viewed in the light

---

[1] ibid., pp. 39–41.   [2] ibid., pp. 40–1.   [3] ibid., p. 42.
[4] Theodor Haecker, *Soren Kierkegaard*, p. 16.
[5] Vide E. L. Allen, op. cit., p. 190, and H. R. Mackintosh, *Types of Modern Theology*, Nisbet, London, 1937, p. 28.

of the *Postscript*. There the problem of the *Fragments* is described
as 'an introduction-problem not to Christianity but to becoming
a Christian'.[1] It seems indubitable, then, that the point of talking
about the Paradox in the *Fragments* is that it is an answer to the
question which was Kierkegaard's great question, namely 'What
does it mean for me to become a Christian?' An instance of this
is the assertion that all that is required of contemporary testimony
is that it be said 'We have believed that in such and such a year
God appeared among us in the humble form of a servant'.[2] The
expressions 'offence' and 'absurd' which are used here with
such emphasis recall the Gospels and the Fathers. Later, in
Training in Christianity, they were said to be specifically Christian
categories.[3]

The problem of the *Fragments* is restated with greater force
in the *Postscript* where Kierkegaard maintains that Christianity
is a relation of subjectivity towards a paradox.

> 'When subjectivity, inwardness, is the truth, the truth
> becomes objectively a paradox; and the fact that the truth
> is objectively a paradox shows in its turn that subjectivity
> is the truth. For the objective situation is repellent; and
> the expression for the objective repulsion constitutes the
> tension and the measure of the corresponding inwardness.'[4]

We see here the truth of Lindström's thesis, as against Bohlin's,
that there can be no separation between the two themes of
subjectivity and paradox. The paradox is what corresponds to
subjectivity. Here Kierkegaard reverses the psychological method
and reads off from the objective constituent the nature of the
'subjective' relation. Since the object of faith is a paradox then
the attempt to approach this absurdum 'objectively' by the way
of approximation is doomed to failure.[5] This way of approximation, the way of objective or disinterested enquiry which
approximates to certainty or a high degree of probability, was
precisely what Socrates shunned.[6] The mistake it makes is that
of assuming that it is the right way of dealing with this, whereas
the absurd cannot be handled objectively at all. Kierkegaard
compares it with Overskou's comedy *Misunderstanding upon*

---

[1] *Postscript*, p. 340.   [2] *Fragments*, p. 87.   [3] *Training in Christianity*, p. 83.
[4] *Postscript*, p. 183.   [5] ibid., p. 188.   [6] ibid.

Misunderstanding.[1] The way of approximation does indeed pile misunderstanding upon misunderstanding because it would make the absurd probable—which it cannot be ; and it would substitute historical knowledge for the attitude of faith. Then the question of the validity of Christianity becomes a simple matter of the truth of a historical statement. But the whole point is that the Paradox can only be a historical statement ' by virtue of the absurd '. That is to say, it is because it is historical this Paradox is the Paradox and the absurd. To say that it is purely historical is to gloss over the paradox and play down its absurdity. This point is driven home with all of Kierkegaard's biting irony. The objective seeker, he says ' has in fact learned something else about faith than when he believed ; he has learned that he no longer believes, since he almost knows, or as good as knows, or extremely and emphatically almost knows '.[2] If there is certainty in the matter what is certain is not what the theologian wants to be certain.[3] Kierkegaard contends that the Hegelian thinkers wanted to dissolve the paradox by saying that viewed eternally it was not a paradox.

> ' If speculative philosophy wishes to . . . say there is no paradox when the matter is viewed eternally, divinely, theocentrically . . . then I admit that I am not in a position to determine whether the speculative philosopher is right, for I am only a poor existing human being, not competent to contemplate the eternal either eternally or divinely or theocentrically, but compelled to content myself with existing.'[4]

We see here the ' existential ' quality of Kierkegaard's polemic against Hegel. According to this the Hegelian interpretation errs in two respects. (i) It assumes wrongly that the philosopher has powers of knowledge which somehow transcend those of ordinary people insofar as he is able to view things from the vantage-point of eternity. In point of fact, however, we are all able to know only what is presented to us in our experience. (ii) It also mistakes the character of the object of faith, making it simple and not complex. It is not a matter of making a metaphysical

[1] ibid., p. 189.　　　　　　　　　　　　　　[2] ibid.
[3] ibid., p. 190.　　　　　　　　　　　　　　[4] ibid.

assertion. Merely to map a dialectic, however commendable it may be as a piece of logic, will not suffice. For the Paradox is a fact. And this factual element is essential for the religious use of the assertion. The Paradox is the object of religious faith because it is such that it evokes a decision,[1] and its ethical significance as the Pattern or Paradigm is utterly dependent on the factual element. This is an important point which we shall see discussed in *Training in Christianity* as the ' offence of the Paradox '.

Training in Christianity takes up the themes of Paradox and offence in a sharper and more polemical way. The point that Kierkegaard wished to emphasise was the offence and risk of believing in One whose humiliation during His life on earth was a terrible reality. He insists that the concept of offence is a characteristic note of Christianity in exactly the same way as that of faith is also characteristic, and that the two concepts are indeed closely related.[2] For it is the possibility of offence that makes it necessary to choose either faith or offence.

> ' Offence has essentially to do with the composite term God and Man, or with the God-Man. Speculation naturally had the notion that it ' comprehended ' the God-Man—this one can easily comprehend, for speculation in speculating about the God-Man leaves out temporal existence. . . . No, the *situation* is inseparable from the God-Man. The God-Man is not the unity of God and mankind. Such terminology exhibits the profundity of optical illusion. The God-Man is unity of God and an individual man '.[3]

So the offence κατ' ἐξοχήν has to do with the God-Man. It can take one of two forms—the offence of loftiness or the offence of lowliness.[4] The first is the offence at the contradiction that an individual lowly man acts in a way that suggests he is God.[5] Kierkegaard illustrates this ' offence which has to do with Loftiness ' by reference to two passages of Scripture—Matthew XI, 6 (the answer to John the Baptist's query whether He was the Messiah), and John VI, 61 (Jesus' declaration that He is the living bread). The picture of Jesus that Kierkegaard thus draws

---

[1] Cp. ibid., pp. 201ff. and p. 188.
[2] *Training in Christianity*, p. 83.
[3] ibid., pp. 83–4.   [4] ibid., p. 84.   [5] ibid, p. 99.

I

for us is as far as possible historically correct. It is the opinion
of most New Testament scholars that Jesus Himself thought that
He was the Son of God, that He acted in such a way as to suggest
that He was God.[1] So Kierkegaard rightly says that it is ' Jesus
Christ Himself who calls attention to the possibility of offence '.[2]
The second kind of offence—that of lowliness—is in a way the
reverse of the first. Here one is not offended by the claim for the
man but rather by what the claim does for God, by ' the observation that God is this man—whether one is now about to believe
that He is God, or is merely pondering reflectively over this
infinite self-contradiction that God should be such a man '.[3] Jesus
was impotent, poor and suffering—and at the time of His cruci-
fixion the disciples found it very difficult to believe that He was
the Messiah. 'All were offended in Him, literally all! ' ' But if
there were need of any proof of the fact that the possibility of
the offence belongs essentially to the experience of faith, it is
exhibited here : all were offended in Him.' This is the point
that Kierkegaard makes again and again in *Training in Christianity*,
that faith and the offensive paradox are, as it were, the two sides
of the same penny. If one is to believe one cannot at all avoid
the possibility of offence. For believing means having faith and
faith implies the possibility of the offence, and means that we
go through this possibility to the blessed acceptance of this
humble man as God.[4] The challenge which the Paradox must
have for us is described in an entry in the Journal of 1849 :

> ' The opposite of antiquity which used the third person
> of itself, because one's life was merely a fact, is to risk
> everything by saying " I ", to say the highest thing about

---

[1] Cp. Wm. Manson, *Jesus the Messiah*, Hodder & Stoughton, 1943, pp. 5 f. et
passim. Vide also his *Commentary on Luke's Gospel*, pp. xxiii ff. et passim.
Even if, however, we accept the conclusion of such a theologian as Bultmann that
we have no actual logia of Jesus to this effect (*Theology of the New Testament*, pp. 9 f.,
26 f., 51) the point concerning offence is not at all changed. Indeed Bultmann seems
to think that he is enabling us to see this more clearly. (*Kerygma and Myth*, S.P.C.K.,
1953, p. 44.) The offence at the claim that Jesus *was* God remains even for Bultmann
though he may describe it as necessary mythology. The radical criticism which
leaves us no knowledge of the historical Jesus (cf. J. Knox and P. Tillich—' the
picture of Jesus as the Christ in the New Testament ') does not essentially change
the truth of Kierkegaard's view.

[2] *Training in Christianity*, p. 104.

[3] ibid., p. 107.

[4] Cp. ibid., pp. 100, 106, 107, 122, 140, 141.

oneself directly. That is expressed in the God-Man if he
were great in such a way as to become a third person.'[1]

Since He is not thus great, He confronts us as a challenging
'Thou' to our 'I', and it is this challenge that demands faith.[2]
Further, since faith alone can assert that He is the God-Man we
can say that the Paradox exists only for faith.[3]

This is the doctrine of the Absolute Paradox in its outlines.
There are important elements developed by Kierkegard which
we shall discuss later. Meantime it is best that we should deal
with the interpretation of what has been described. Reuter's
theory of the Hegelian origin of the idea of Paradox proved very
important for Kierkegaard scholarship because it was taken up
by the two Scandinavian scholars Bohlin and Geismar. They
adopted this thesis and developed it into a criticism of the way
Kierkegaard talks about the Paradox. Geismar is not as definite
and extreme as Bohlin who says quite emphatically that the
discussion is vitiated by what he calls the intellectualism Kierkegaard reveals here. The argument is that in order to secure more
favourable conditions for aiming a death-blow at Hegel's interpretation of the nature of Christianity Kierkegaard took over
Hegel's premises. His polemic against Hegel's attempt to dissolve the contradiction of the God-Man, therefore, adopts the
Hegelian categories and metaphysical distinctions. This results,
says Bohlin, in an ambiguous attitude towards Hegelianism.

'This involves that however emphatically Kierkegaard
has asserted the irrational character of Christianity against
the intellectualism of Hegel's conception of religion,
irrationalism with him includes a marked intellectualistic
element. And this is the reason why Kierkegaard also,
despite the strong emphasizing of the historical revelation,
has not been able to avoid spiritualising the latter, not
indeed like Hegel into a general Christ-principle, but to a
paradox in which man knows himself to be absolutely
separate from God.'[4]

For Bohlin this ambiguous relation to the Hegelian philosophy

---

[1] *Journals*, 975.   [2] *Training in Christianity*, p. 143.
[3] ibid., p. 122. Cp. *Philosophical Fragments*, p. 80.
[4] Bohlin, op. cit., pp. 435–6.

leads to an abstract metaphysical conception of the religious problem, to the completely Hegelian idea of a synthesis of the finite and the infinite. The treatment of the doctrine of Christ's Person is metaphysical and not ethical.[1] This complaint of Bohlin's is very strange, and it must be rejected for three reasons. First, it is quite wrong to say that Kierkegaard understands the Paradox in a Hegelian way as a synthesis of finite and infinite. The *Postscript* and *Training in Christianity* are quite definite on the point that it is the historicity of the God-Man that makes it a paradox of an absolute kind. Indeed Kierkegaard even defines the paradox as being this : that ' God has existed in human form, has been born, has grown up '.[2] The second point is that it is wrong, as we have seen in connection with the ideas of subjectivity and the leap, to call Kierkegaard an ' irrationalist '. Here is the root of Bohlin's criticism, and in this his method of interpretation is at fault. For the trouble arises because he characterises Kierkegaard in an *a priori* fashion as irrationalist and then complains because he is not. Surely this is just another instance (to borrow Berkeley's phrase) of kicking up the dust and then complaining because we cannot see. Kierkegaard was no irrationalist—any more than he was some other ' -ist '. He probably realised better than most people of his age that it is no business of the thinker to take sides but simply to describe and criticise a way of speaking. Thus here he was anxious to describe as fully as he could the peculiar object of Christian faith. He saw that it was a Paradox but he wanted to show how paradoxical it was.[3] This brings us to our last point against Bohlin. It is difficult to express this, because it is a matter of saying ' Yes, but what of it? ' It is surely trivial to say of any theology that there is an intellectualistic element in it even though it may be the theology of the profoundest mysticism—like St. Bernard's of Clairvaux. The point is that in so far as any religious attitude involves concepts

---

[1] ibid., pp. 453, 494, 526. Geismar makes essentially the same point (*Søren Kierkegaard*, vol. III, p. 78). ' Not only has Kierkegaard made the Athanasia, doctrine accepted by reason : he has made belief identical with the acceptance of the dogma.'

[2] *Postscript*, p. 194.

[3] It is this, I think, that Geismar probably had in mind when he talked about the intellectualism of the theory of the Paradox. However he too, like Bohlin stresses too much the ' critique of reason ' as, for instance, when he talks of ' the defiant attitude towards human reason ' which Søren Kierkegaard displays in this matter of the Paradox (op. cit. III, p. 69).

and these are being described there must be an intellectualistic element in our talk. To complain of this, however, is to make a very strange statement. It would be like saying that a person who says that $4+10 = 15$ and $5+6 = 10$ is really being very intellectualistic because he presupposes the addibility of numbers. Should someone tell us that $4+10$ was equivalent to 15 either we would say that he was giving the number fifteen a new meaning or else that he could not count. If, however, we went on to ask him whether $3 \times 5 = 15$ and he agreed then it would become clear that he was not giving the number fifteen a new use (the use would have included a theory about the value of o). This becomes even clearer when he says that $5+6 = 10$. By this time there is no question in our mind and we say that he just cannot count or that he is talking nonsense. It is, however, quite unnatural to say that he is being an intellectualistic irrationalist. The charge of intellectualism which Bohlin brings forward cannot, then, be sustained. Ruttenbeck, who also criticises it, gives other reasons for rejecting it. For him the theology of paradox has its roots in Kierkegaard's life,[1] and he argues vigorously against the charge of intellectualism brought forward by Bohlin and Geismar.

‘ In so far as this is existential thought it is before God and thus a believing thought. As such, it has its limits in reality, in the divine gift ; it analyses this reality according to its laws, it does not destroy it. On the contrary, its labour is put to the service of reality, to the service of revelation, and it is in it that the objectivity of belief finds its best guarantee. And, insofar as thought hurls itself incessantly to reality it becomes aware of reality. The paradox is the sign of reality. . . . Thought, as believing thought, takes part in the struggle of belief.’[2]

The meaning of this argument is not entirely clear, but the final point is linked closely with the third reason we adduced above for rejecting Bohlin's thesis. Ruttenbeck makes a very interesting comment on this thesis when he reminds us that it had been hinted at by Rasmus Nielsen (1809–1884) who had been a disciple of

---

[1] Ruttenbeck, op. cit., p. 356.
[2] ibid., p. 360.

Kierkegaard's but later broke from him.[1] In 1869 he published his *Philosophy of Religion*, where he argues that mystery is to be distinguished from paradox, that mystery in fact ' destroys the contradiction, dissolving the opposed terms '.[2] It seems difficult to distinguish this from the heresy of monophysitism, and on this ground it can hardly be said to be a better description of the Christian theology of Incarnation than Kierkegaard's. It is also interesting to recall that Kierkegaard had said of Nielsen :

> ' He is not a dialectician and he has not even got an idea of what the passion of belief is. . . . A policeman's eye discovers the falsification at once. All his position is outside dialectical passion.'[3]

We can now see that the position, which has been argued for by Bohlin and Geismar amongst Scandinavian scholars, and which Emmanuel Hirsch also supported in his *Kierkegaard-Studien* cannot be accepted. The charge of intellectualistic anti-rationalism is therefore false. However, it raises a question which we have not as yet answered. Did Kierkegaard understand his Absolute Paradox to be a contradiction (*contra rationem*) or a non-logical suprarational paradox (*supra rationem*)? To this we turn next.

There are many reputable Kierkegaard scholars who say that the Paradox in Kierkegaard is *supra rationem*. For instance, Theodor Haecker is very emphatic on this point. He expresses his concern at the use of this word ' Paradox ' by Kierkegaard and his equally liberal use of the word ' absurd '. He would prefer the use of the former term, because he regards the latter as having only one meaning for God and man, and that is irrationality. It denotes ' the abrogation of the principle of contradiction, the denial of the principle of identity '.[4] Haecker recognises that there is a strong flavour of paradox in all religious language and says this is as it should be :

---

[1] ibid., p. 354. Cp. Lowrie, *Kierkegaard*, p. 381. ' Søren Kierkegaard's sense of the need of making himself understood . . . prompted him . . . in 1849 to " draw " to him Rasmus Nielsen, Professor of Philosophy in the University. In fact, the Professor had already shown that he was eager to be drawn, and in the end he justified Kierkegaard's saying that a disciple is the greatest of all calamities.' Vide *Journals* 1182 where Kierkegaard describes Nielsen's ' advances ' and ibid. 1220— ' The whole Rasmus Nielsen episode was a grief to me.'

[2] R. Nielsen, *Philosophy of Religion*, pp. 11, 33, 62.

[3] *Papirer* XI A 349.

[4] Theodor Haecker, *Kierkegaard—the Cripple*, London, Harvill Press, 1948, p. 22.

' The genuine paradox is a form of honourable acknow-
ledgement, on the part of human understanding, of the
majesty of the divine mysteries, and of the fact that His ways
are not our ways. It is an expression of the otherwise
indefinable relation between finite man and the infinite
creator. . . . But the paradox is far from being an absurdity.
This metaphysical misunderstanding is truly lamentable.'[1]

This comment of Haecker's is very interesting, because it seems
to admit, on the one hand, for Kierkegaard the terms ' Paradox '
and ' the Absurd ' are synonymous whilst saying, on the other
hand, that what Kierkegaard means to say is that Christ is the
Paradox which is not absurd.   Haecker's views are very much
like Geismar's who argues that from the very beginning Kierkegaard means by the term ' Paradox ' ' not the anti-rational but
the discontinuous, that which comes as an absolutely new
beginning '.[2]   The evidence that Geismar produces in support of
this contention is the passage in the *Papirer*, where Kierkegaard
says that, when he distinguishes between Philosophy and Christianity by drawing the distinction between mediation and Paradox,
he is making the same point as Leibniz made :

' What I am accustomed to express in this way : that
Christianity lies in the Paradox, Philosophy in Mediation,
Leibniz also expresses by making the distinction between
what is above Reason and what is against Reason.   Belief
is above Reason.   By Reason he understands, as he says many
times, a chaining together (enchainement) of truth, a conclusion from reasons.   Belief cannot therefore be demonstration, proof or understanding . . . and what will this say other
than that this is a Paradox ; for this is clearly the distinguishing mark of the Paradox—it lacks continuity, or at any
rate only has an inverted continuity, which means that it
does not originally show itself as a continuity.'[3]

It does not seem to us that this is very good evidence for the
particular point that Geismar wants to make.   Indeed this is an

[1] ibid., pp. 23–4.
[2] Geismar, op. cit., vol III, p. 71.
[3] *Papirer* IV C 29.   The reference is to Leibniz's *Théodicée*, Hanover und Leipzig
1736, pp. 31 f., 66, 70 f.

instance of the confusion of the two senses of the term ' Paradox '
which we distinguished at the outset. Therefore, whilst we agree
that this shows how anxious Kierkegaard was to distinguish but
not oppose faith and reason, there is no ground afforded by
this quotation for saying that the Absolute Paradox is not a
contradiction. However, there is a great deal of material in the
Papirer which could be quoted in favour of this view, and we
must examine this carefully.

The first piece of evidence from the *Papirer* is the brief remark
in 1849 that there is a view of the word such that the paradox
is regarded as above every system.[1] Eleven years later when he
was reading Helfferich's *Die Christliche Mystik* he came across a
reference to Hugo de St. Victor's statement of the relation of faith
to reason. This is the comment he made on it :

> ' This statement of Hugo de St. Victor is correct : " In
> fact, with regard to things that are above reason faith is not
> supported by reason, because faith does not at all understand
> what it yet believes with all its power. But there again is
> something which determines reason, or by which reason is
> determined, to hold faith in honour, and this faith it cannot
> understand fully." This is the principle which I myself have
> developed (e.g. in the *Postscript*) : that every absurdity is
> not " the absurd " or the paradox. Reason's work consists
> exactly in a negative knowledge of the paradox—nothing
> more.
>
> In an earlier entry of the *Journal*[2] (when I was reading
> Aristotle's *Rhetoric*) I wrote that instead of dogmatics one
> should introduce a Christian rhetoric. It ought to be related
> to πίστις : πίστις in classical Greek indicates a conviction
> (more than δόξη opinion) which has for its object what is
> likely. But Christianity, which upsets all the rational man's
> ideas and inverts his values, puts πίστις in relation to the
> unlikely. This concept of the unlikely, the absurd, ought then
> to be the theme to develop, because it would be believed
> that in the realm of absurd things all kinds of absurdity are
> equal. No, the concept of the absurd is strictly this : to

[1] *Journals*, 282.
[2] Vide, VI A 17, 19.

understand that one cannot understand. A negative category, but as dialectical as all other positive categories. The absurd, the paradox is constructed in such a way that in fact reason could not by its own power reduce it to nonsense and show its emptiness. No ; it is a sign, an enigma faced with which reason can only say : " I cannot resolve it ; for me that is not intelligible." But it does not follow therefrom that the paradox is in fact nonsense. But we see that if we abolish faith completely reason becomes presumptuous and will dare conclude " ergo the paradox is nonsense ". . . . Faith believes in the Paradox, it believes the Paradox. Let us say then, to quote Hugo de St. Victor's words that " reason can well allow itself be determined to honour faith" for it gains profundity by the negative category of the Paradox.'[1]

Three years after this was written he returned to the *Postscript* and makes clear what he had wanted to say there :

' There is a double point contained in the *Postscript*.

A. In the most rigorous Christian sense there ought not to be a Christian knowledge. In every case the Christian thinker ought to ask faith's permission to be occupied wth knowledge, the latter being not its superior but its inferior. This is not at all a new principle, it is the very principle of Christianity. . . . The *Postscript* rightly moves from faith to faith, to the existential and not to speculation. . . . If someone cannot be content with simple faith . . . he will find something higher : the martyr. . . . From the Christian point of view it is the only way to " go further " than faith. . . . And if someone wants to occupy himself with knowledge and has some aptitude for it, no objections at all will be made. . . . But if knowledge sets itself to declare that it cannot stop at faith, that it must " go further "—to speculation as the higher goal, then I think that the existential security police must intervene. . . . This is the importance

---

[1] *Papirer* X 2 A 354. The translation of the clause ' because faith does not understand ' is not too sure because the editors suggest that for the text's ' Troen ikke fatter ' we should read ' Forften ikke fatter '. If this is so then the translation would be ' reason does not understand '.

of the *Postscript*. Its reaction towards knowledge is carried through logically . . .

.   .   .   .

.   .   .   .

B. If there must be a Christian knowledge this cannot be based on the principle that faith must be understood; but on this principle, that it must be understood that faith cannot be understood. . . .'[1]

In the same volume of the *Papirer* there is the unpublished 'Reply to Theophilus Nicolaus' of which two points are here relevant—(i) that the Paradox is the negative criterion of faith in so far as it stops reason.[2] (ii) the Paradox is the negative criterion of what is above understanding.[3] This completes the evidence and we are now able to appreciate that in all this there is nothing that refutes the assertion that logically speaking the Paradox is a contradiction. What Geismar rightly points to is the fact that for Kierkegaard one of the most important things that the theory of Paradox implies was that 'belief' could not be assimilated to 'understanding'. Thus he says that the Paradox is discontinuous, by which he presumably means that it is no result of argumentation. Here lies the force of Kierkegaard's attack on Hegel in that he sees that the Paradox cannot be made a part of a philosophical system. It is not the bad expression of a useful idea; it is the only expression of something more than idea. In this way too the Paradox can be said to indicate the discontinuous —it indicates a new point of departure for life.[4] But this very use presupposes the view that the Paradox is absurd. Thus in *Training in Christianity* Kierkegaard says quite explicitly that the contradiction within the Paradox is what constitutes the possibility of offence which is the religious and ethical value of the Paradox.[5]

The Paradox *sensu strictissimo* is that 'God has existed in human form, has been born and has grown up',[6] and this is a paradox that can in no wise be removed, dissolved or surmounted.[7] For Christian thinking this is therefore its perennial problem— how to understand the Paradox *qua* paradox. It is clear that the

---

[1] *Papirer* X 6 B 114, pp. 144–5.   [2] ibid. B. 68.   [3] ibid. B. 80.
[4] Cp. Geismar, *Lectures on the Religious Thought of Søren Kierkegaard*, p. 63.
[5] *Training in Christianity*, p. 99. Cp. pp. 112, 134.   [6] *Postscript*, p. 194. Cp. p. 191.
[7] ibid., pp. 196–7.

only attitude to it apart from rejection is faith. This means that when one becomes a Christian one accepts that the very centre of one's doctrine is a contradiction. Outside of faith it is regarded as nonsense : only to faith does it reveal its depth of meaning. We have seen that this is what Kierkegaard says in *Training in Christianity*, and an entry early in the *Journal* of 1850 makes the same point. Under the title ' The Absurd ', he says :

> ' The " immediate " believer cannot apprehend the thought that the content of faith is, for the reason and for the third person who is not a believer, the absurd, and that to become a believer everyone must be alone with the absurd. . . . To understand that to the reason it is the absurd, to speak of it thus quite calmly to a third person, admitting that it is the absurd, enduring the burden of the other man looking upon it as the absurd—and nevertheless to believe it. While naturally it is a matter of course that for him who believes it is not the absurd.'[1]

Now wherein lies the absurdity of the Paradox? For Kierkegaard it was in the fact that it was said of a particular human being that he was God.[2] The two terms ' temporal ' and ' eternal ' are for him mutually exclusive or at least qualitatively different. It is sometimes said that the difference between God and man is not absolute, and that it is the mistake of thinking it is so that accounts for the difficulty or absurdity which the Incarnation is for both Kierkegaard and Karl Barth. All the so-called liberal theologians have made some such remark. Thus the late Archbishop William Temple said that ' Christ is God—not generically but identically. Christ is man—not generically but inclusively '.[3] This epigram is attractive but hardly sufficient. It is at least an extremely vague statement ; and seems both to protest against and to be dominated by the misleading idea of the two *natures*. Whatever the point of the statement was its essential weakness can be seen when it is interpreted as saying that Christ as God includes man. The picture that this evokes at once is Euler's

---

[1] *Journals*, 1084.
[2] There is also the contradiction due to sin but this is not relevant here.
[3] The words are really a quotation from Moberley, *Atonement and Personality*, p. xx, which Temple thinks are an admirable summary of the *unity* of Christ's person. Vide : *Foundations* by Seven Oxford Men, Macmillan, 1913, p. 247.

diagram of the relation of class-inclusion such as we have in
All S is P :

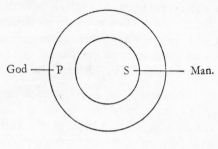

Christ = God ——————⟨ Man-Christ

This is surely wrong.   For this is to miss the whole point of
talking about an Incarnation. ' The Word became flesh.' How
matter-of-fact it sounds—and it is supposed to. Because Kierkegaard starts with the historicity of Jesus Christ, his whole interpretation is in the tradition of the New Testament.   Here is a
man, he says, who was born and grew up like any other Jew of
that epoch. Now the point about this man is that he was God—
Immanuel.   God is usually conceived as omnipresent, omnipotent and omniscient. Because of his very humanity Jesus could
not be any of these. Certainly there is no evidence that he was
either omnipotent or omniscient.[1] This reveals the paradox in
all its perplexity. How are we to think of Christ? It is difficult
for us to imagine what His life was like. It is not because we do
not know what He said or did on so many occasions, but rather
something more subtle. How can we say that He lived as a man
and yet was God? Kierkegaard's Paradox can be seen better if
we talk in terms of historical fact. Was Christ a historical fact?
It is a fact that He lived, but it is not a fact in the *same* sense that
He was God. Contrast the assertion ' Jesus of Nazareth is the
name of a first century Jew and He was God ' with the assertion
' John Jones is five feet six and is a good boxer '. In the latter
case we are asserting two facts that can be verified. Even the

[1] Cp. Mackintosh, *The Person of Christ*, Clark, Edinburgh, 1912. ' The evangelists
nowhere seek to prove Jesus' manhood ; it is for them a tacit and self-evident
assumption. He is revealed to us within the lines and dimensions of human experience. . . . Jesus' bodily and mental life plainly followed the rules of natural
human development ' (p. 10). ' We cannot speak of His omniscience except as we
desert the sources ' (p. 13). He quotes Mark xiii, 32. Cp. too Borchert, *The Original
Jesus*, London, Lutterworth Press, 1933, p. 55.

judgment as to his boxing ability can be easily settled when we see Jones at work in the ring. However, in the first instance it is only one such verifiable fact that we assert. The other part of the sentence is a fact in the sense that we would say that it is ' true ' but its truth is a very different affair from the truth of the first part. This is the contradiction, that of saying that a fact is also not a fact, that a human life is the period in which God Himself was fully revealed.[1] By his insistence on the contradiction in the Paradox Kierkegaard made two things crystal clear. The first was that any philosophical scheme which interpreted Christianity so that the central Christian dogma became a philosophical principle was a complete misrepresentation of the Incarnation doctrine. The second point was that since the Incarnation is thus paradoxical then it cannot be understood and indeed is not supposed to be. The *meaning* of the Incarnation is the religious and moral use.[2] Thus Geismar points out that the important question about the Incarnation for Kierkegaard is the existential meaning of the doctrine.

' It is an indisputable fact that Kierkegaard presents the Christian faith in the person of Jesus Christ as true man and true God, in full conformity with the orthodox Athanasian need. This doctrine of the God-Man is for him the Absolute Paradox. But the important question for Kierkegaard is the existential meaning of this doctrinal content. How does the Paradox determine the mode of existence of the Christian?

Negatively, the paradoxical element in Christianity is a protest against every merely intellectual assimilation, every attempt to regard it as something to understand or explain. . . . The only entrance to Christianity is by way of a practical experience of profound pathos, in which the individual yields himself absolutely in a devotion analogous to the devotion of a woman's love.

Positively it signifies in my view three things : the forgiveness of sins a new point of departure for the moral life ; the absolute obligation to follow Christ in obedience ; the life of Christ as the ideal by which I measure my own departure from perfection and by which I evoke the judgment upon my own imperfection.'[3]

---

[1] Cp. Barth, *Epistle to the Romans*.
[2] Cp. *Postscript*, pp. 191, 192, 197, 288, 290.
[3] Geismar, *Lectures on the Religious Thought of Søren Kierkegaard*, pp. 63f.

In his treatment of the Paradox Kierkegaard makes two important points concerning the Christian doctrine of the Person of Christ. The first is that the divine character of His person could not have been obvious. He makes this point in two ways—by saying (*a*) that the Paradox exists only for faith[1]; (*b*) that Christ was God incognito.[2] It is natural to assume that had one been a contemporary of Jesus Christ one would have been in a better position to recognise Him for what He was. This, Kierkegaard points out, is quite wrong. What He was could not be directly perceived—you do not perceive a contradiction. It has become very fashionable in theology to decry the old distinctions between the ' Jesus of history ' and the ' Christ of faith '.[3] It is therefore ironic to recollect that this is due in part to Kierkegaard who both drew the distinction and opposed the liberal idea of the Jesus of history. Typical of the attitude of theologians (a few years ago at any rate) towards this distinction is this remark of Dr. L. W. Grensted :

> ' The dilemma " Jesus or Christ ", though it was discussed with a certain academic fury a few years ago, and though certain gnostics seem to have done their best with it in the second century, has never had much importance in Christian thinking.'[4]

Now it may well be that the question ' Jesus or Christ? ' has never been very important in Christian thinking. Indeed one might say that Dr. Grensted's remark could not be more true, since it is a tautology. Precisely because it is Christian thinking it will never regard the question as important, indeed will perhaps not see that it can be asked ; for to it Jesus is Christ. This, however, is not to say that the question can never be asked, that it is an impossible question, or that it is meaningless. On the contrary, it has great meaning ; and one of the values of Kierke-

---

[1] *Fragments*, pp. 80, 84, 85. *Postscript*, pp. 189, 191. *Training*, pp. 122, 142–3.

[2] *Training*, pp. 127, 131. *Journals*, 417, 975. *Postscript*, p. 42.

[3] Vide, for instance, J. Mackay, *Preface to Theology*, Nisbet, London, 1942, p. 72, and J. V. L. Casserley, op. cit., p. 231. Both say that it is a false distinction. Mackay says : ' The original Jesus cannot be found by any scientific study or critical approach. . . . We cannot by any conceivable means reach the purely historical Jesus, for the simple reason that such a being does not exist in the New Testament.' But this does not imply that the distinction is false. Then Casserley says that the Jesus of history is a hypothetical figure because the hypothesis insists that He must have been quite unlike the ' Christ of faith '. This is a perfectly wild statement.

[4] L. W. Grensted, *The Person of Christ*, Nisbet, London, 1933, p. 23.

gaard's doctrine of Paradox is that it shows how the distinction is a valid one and it shows too the context in which it is made. The person who was born in Bethlehem (or was it Nazareth?), who lived in Galilee and died on a cross outside Jerusalem in A.D. 26—he was an ordinary human figure. True, he must have been a startling figure in many ways, disconcerting and holy—yet a man, for all that. He could be seen, touched and so on. There was no doubt that he was real. If now we say that he was God how do we know? It is not a matter of his having been so good and kind that out of respect to Him we say, We'll call Him God ; because by definition He could never be good enough. If he is a man then we cannot imagine him sufficiently good for it to be obvious that He is God. Thus Kierkegaard says that Jesus Christ is God incognito. He dwelt among us and ' the world knew Him not '. Kierkegaard describes the abiding character of the Paradox thus :

> ' The coming of Christ is and remains a paradox. To his contemporaries the paradox lay in the fact that he, this particular individual man who looked like other men, spoke like them, followed their habits and customs, was the son of God. To later generations the paradox is different ; for as they do not see him with their physical eye it is easier to imagine him as the Son of God, and then that which gives offence and scandal is that he adopted the habit of mind of a man of a particular age.'[1]

The very historicity of Jesus therefore makes it impossible that anyone who was his contemporary should directly perceive his divinity, and impossible too that any succeeding generation should discover his divinity in the way in which it could discover the goodness of St. Francis of Assisi. It is indeed true that the Gospels start from this assertion and declare themselves to be the history of the Son of God. However, this assertion is not made on the basis of historical evidence, as we have seen. In this way the old distinction between the ' Jesus of history ' and the ' Christ of faith ' holds and is an interesting one. Where the distinction can be at fault is when it is made to mean that there are two persons. There is only one person here. The distinction points

[1] *Journals*, 417.

to the difficulty of recognising Him. The truth about Him, says faith, is that, contrary to all appearance, He was God.

Now if this historical figure is interpreted as the Paradox only by faith and not by an impartial history, it is then true to say with Kierkegaard that the Paradox only exists for faith. This is a tautology, but an interesting one and by no means empty and useless. It brings home to us again the important point that the Paradox is known by faith and that you cannot make it pure history and still expect it to be the figure that the Christian religion is concerned to find and preserve. Talking of Jesus as God, says Dr. Grensted, is ' an assertion of that which is implicit in worship.'[1] This is not at all trivial. It is necessary that we should remember this statement's context lies in worship. Therefore, when the writers of the New Testament talk about what Jesus said and did they were doing something extremely different from what a biographer does when he talks of the person whose life he describes. There may be an analogy insofar as the biographer may admire the hero of his tale. Yet there is a tremendous difference. His documents bring him the evidence for all his valuation. The New Testament was written because people knew that in Jesus God had Himself come into their lives. Grensted's remark characterizes with precision this attitude. It is not surprising, then, that the New Testament writers lay a great, an almost exclusive stress on this faith-attitude. Thus Ritschl observes that in spite of Jesus' new commandment of love only very sparing use is made in the New Testament of the conception of love to Christ—and this for good reasons.

> ' As a generic idea love to Christ is more indefinite than faith in Him. The former term leaves it undecided whether we put ourselves on a level with Christ or subordinate ourselves to Him. But faith in Christ includes the confession of His Godhead and His dominion over us, and thus shuts out the possibility of equality with Him.[2]'

By his insistence on the fact that the God-Man is the Absolute Paradox Kierkegaard safeguards the interpretation of our attitude to Him. Because it is Paradox that we have here we are con-

[1] Grensted, op. cit., p. 244.
[2] Ritschl, *Justification and Reconciliation*, Clark, Edinburgh, 1900, pp. 593–4.

fronted with something we cannot understand, something we must accept. Faith is not thus a simple matter of feeling one way or another—there is a core of doctrine. On the other hand, because this doctrine is related to the person's mode of existence it cannot be something that demands simply an effort of understanding. Therefore once more the ethical or ethico-religious meaning of the Paradox becomes clear.

One way in which Kierkegaard brings out this ethico-religious use of the Paradox is by means of his idea of contemporaneity. He was one of the first to point out that an interesting feature of Christian faith is that it is a present relation to a past historical figure. Thus he says in the *Philosophical Fragments* that the object of faith is the contemporary.[1] There he discusses ' the disciple at second hand ' and shows that he is not at all less fortunately situated than the disciple at first hand.

> ' The contemporary learner enjoys one advantage, which
> the learner of a later generation alas! will doubtless greatly
> envy him, if only for the sake of doing something. A con-
> temporary may go where he can see the Teacher—and may
> he then believe his eyes? Why not? But may he also believe
> that this makes him a disciple? By no means. If he believes
> his eyes he is deceived, for God is not immediately knowable.
> But then perhaps he may shut his eyes. Just so ; but if he
> does, what profit does he have from his contemporaneity?[2]

The point is that Jesus' historical contemporaries were only better situated than we are in the sense that they saw the person whom we know by report. They had first-hand knowledge and we have documentary evidence. However, this has nothing to do with Christianity, because this direct knowledge even could not reveal to them the secret that He was God. This means that in so far as ' Christian experience ' or Christian faith is concerned that the contemporaries were no better situated than we are. Now Kierkegaard calls this faith-relation contemporareousness. The man who knows Christ, has faith in Him, is contemporaneous with Him no matter to what generation or age he belongs. He explains this by saying that in regard to the eternal the only tense possible is the present (which is reminiscent of Boethius' defini-

[1] *Philosophical Fragments*, pp. 84–5.   [2] ibid., p. 51.

K

tion of eternity as a constant present). It is rather unfortunate
that he should give this obvious and too metaphysical reason
for a statement that is rich in meaning. Hirsch explains Kierkegaard's use and makes no further comment :

> ' Kierkegaard . . . filled the term " contemporaneity "
> with a very concrete sense. The contemporaneity has its
> ground in the presence of the eternal which is equally near
> to every man of every age—the presence that is of the divine
> reconciler. . . . But this reconciler is near to me and to every-
> one in His historical reality.'[1]

One sees here an emphasis that is very popular in contemporary
theology which, in reaction against the distance of Schweitzer's
Historical Jesus, talks of the nearness of Christ, ' the living
Christ '.[2] The picture this suggests is that of an actor on the
Elizabethan stage who appears for a while on the stage and then
for the rest of the time acts in the balcony of the stage. However,
this is not quite the point that Kierkegaard had in mind ; for
there is nothing to suggest that when he talks of the contemporaneity of the believer with Christ, he was thinking of the
Second Person of the Trinity. This idea of the living Christ is
irrelevant here, and we must see how Kierkegaard brings out
what he means in a confused passage we shall now quote :

> ' Christ is . . . not at all a merely historical person, since
> as the Paradox He is an extremely unhistorical person. But
> this is the difference between poetry and reality : contem-
> poraneousness. The difference between poetry and history
> is clearly this, that history is what really occurred, whereas
> poetry is the possible, the imaginary. But what really oc-
> curred (the past) is not (except in a special sense, i.e. in
> contrast with poetry) the real. It lacks the determinant which
> is the determinant of truth (as inwardness) and of all religious-
> ness, the *for thee*. The past is not reality—for me : only
> contemporary is reality for me. What thou dost live con-
> temporaneous with is reality—*for thee*. And thus every man
> can be contemporary only with the age in which he lives—

[1] Hirsch, *Kierkegaard-Studien*, II, p. 80.
[2] Vide T. R. Glover, *Jesus in the Experience of Men*. Grensted, op. cit., pp. 76 ff.
J. S. Whale, *Christian Doctrine*, pp. 11 ff., 98 ff.

and then with one thing more : with Christ's life on earth ;
for Christ's life on earth, sacred history, stands for itself alone
outside history . . . Christ's life on earth is not a past
event. . . . His earthly life possesses an eternal contempora-
neousness.'[1]

This is a very difficult passage and it is to be feared that no
interpretation can be regarded as certain. However, it seems
obvious that Kierkegaard has confused himself by being concerned with the temporal sense of the word ' contemporaneous '
at all. Had he said quite clearly that he was using the word meta-
phorically the sense of the passage would be clearer. As it is,
however, we must proceed in a piece-meal fashion for a moment.
(i) It is true to say that Christ is not at all a merely historical
person if what is meant is that what we want to say about Him
and His life cannot be exhausted by a purely historical description.
By definition He is (to use the old phrase) ' the hypostatic union '
of the historical and the supra-historical. (ii) To say, however,
that Christ's life on earth is not a past event is saying something
more than this. It is not simply to say that the concept ' the life
of Christ on earth ' is an open concept insofar as it cannot be
completely defined (and open in a peculiar way, a way different
from that in which the concept ' person ' or ' my experience ' is
open). It says that this phrase is not making a temporal assertion.
It is then to say that the history of the words and deeds of a person
living during the period 7 B.C. to A.D.26, which is the cash value
of ' the life of Christ on earth ' is not history. This is sheer
contradiction and nonsense. (iii) The ' for thee ' is independent
of the temporal presentation of something which makes that real
to me now. For instance, ' I see a dagger ' says Macbeth, and we
would say that it is real for him. But the ' for him ' here carries
with it a certain connotation of subjectivity which would justify
a John Blunt's saying, ' Why don't you just say straight out that
Macbeth's dagger was an illusion? ' Contrast with this ' Toothache was never real to me till the other night. I woke up with
an awful pain, etc.' The pain was ' real ' only when experienced
then. Now the point is that the Paradox is real in a different sense
from either of these. I think we can now see something of what
Kierkegaard had in mind. We can perhaps express it in a somewhat

[1] *Training in Christianity*, pp. 67–8.

paradoxical way by saying that the assertion that Christ is God incarnate is not a historical judgment. That is, by this statement we at once refer to a person belonging to the past and make a judgment that is no more an assertion about the past than it is about the present—indeed less so. Therefore in a real sense the assertion is timeless. This together with the trivial point that as an assertion of mine (i.e. as a psychological fact) it is made now, would give us grounds for calling it a present relation to the past. But we are far from having exhausted the meaning of this idea, because the further point is that the assertion carries with it certain ethical and religious directives which are essentially prescriptions as to what I should do now. In *this* sense I am presently related to or contemporaneous with the past. After all, then, this mysterious abrogation of the intervening centuries is linked with the doctrinal significance of the Paradox and with the ' existential ' understanding of this significance.

There remains one point that is extremely important for any discussion of the Paradox or of faith in the Incarnation, and that is that for the believer there is no absurdity in the Paradox. Two passages from the *Papirer* are relevant here. One of them we have already quoted : it is that in which Kierkegaard speaks at once of the absurdity of the content of faith to the unbeliever and to reason and of its being quite other than absurd to the believer.[1] Here is something analogous to the immediate knowledge after the break-up of immediacy. The other passage is from the reply to Theophilus Nicolaus :

> ' The absurd is a category ; it is the negative category of the divine and of the relation to God. After the believer believes the absurd is no longer absurd—faith changes it. But any new moment of weakness gives it more or less this character : if it were not thus faith would not be faith, but some kind of knowing. Thus the absurd throws us into faith's sphere which is a sphere apart. For a third person who has no faith the believer commits himself to something foolish. . . . For the absurd and faith make a mutually necessary relation if there must be and if there is to be maintained a friendliness between two so different qualities as God and man. But there is nothing terrifying about this category of

[1] *Journals* 1084.

the absurd. On the contrary, it is the category of courage and enthusiasm. Let us return to the analogy of love. We know that love makes one blind. True. But what a misfortune it is not to be made blind by love. . . . True love blinds completely. It is the same with the health and joy that faith breathes in the bosom of the absurd.'[1]

This is a clear statement of the paradox and believing the Paradox. Obviously it is futile to ask for a belief in something ridiculous. It is impossible to imagine a person saying, ' I believe the moon is a green cheese '—or at any rate if we ever came across someone who said this we would know what to do with him! This is what Kierkegaard has said already ; that just any absurdity is not good enough here. It is an absurd that must be true. It must make sense when we have believed. We have seen quite clearly that the contradiction must not be played down. Here more than anywhere in Christianity we must *believe*. It is usually said of Tertullian that he made the Christian faith a fluid faith in paradox. What is probably the truth is that he grasped this point, that faith believed where it *could not* know. Kierkegaard repeats the salutary lesson that *credo* means *nescio, sed credo quia absurdum est objectum fidei*. This is the leap through the possibility of offence. Once on the other side, though, we see the meaningfulness and truth of the absurd so that it is no longer for us the absurd. This meaning and truth is what we have seen the Paradox involves, namely its ethico-religious use. This is the truth in Ritschl's interpretation of doctrine in terms of value. The lesson we have learned, however, is that the absurd is always a contradiction for the reason which is thought outside of faith while being truth ' for me ' in faith. This is the difference between philosophy and theology. Theology which is ' in the sphere of faith ' will talk of ' the unity of the Person of Christ, the mystery of the Incarnation and the Redemptive Revelation '. Philosophy will be concerned only with seeing (*a*) the absurdity of the Paradox ; (*b*) the new use of the word ' true ' which describes the value of the Paradox in terms of the individual's worship and life.

[1] *Papirer* X 6 A 79.

CHAPTER VI

KIERKEGAARD'S IMPORTANCE

We have now examined both the development and the expression of Kierkegaard's theme of subjectivity. We have seen how it sprang out of certain historical movements both as the result of specific influences and as a protest against a particular natural theology. The time has now come for us to try and formulate our answer to the question, Why is Kierkegaard important now? What is his significance for us in the present state of flux in which philosophy of religion finds itself? The question seems straightforward enough, and yet the answer seems difficult to find. It is difficult to find because it is so tempting to bring out a simple answer. Thus one can say that Kierkegaard was the first modern thinker to realize that the philosopher of religion must take religion seriously. This is obviously inadequate but it is not at all irrelevant or trivial. Clearly, however, making this sort of statement is not enough. We must now take stock of our discussion hitherto and see what we have been able to glean from it. What insights have we seen in Kierkegaard's discussion that give us some assistance in our attempt to deal with religion philosophically? We shall discuss these in terms of what we may call the logic of the religious person's belief in God and the logic of the Christian's belief in Christ. This terminology would have struck Kierkegaard as being very strange, but we are convinced that his thought loses none of its essential value when it is rendered in these terms. Only as we try to cast the insights Kierkegaard expressed in what was often clumsy language into a form which is more intelligible to us now can we see the relevance of his thought. There can be no greater mistake than that which one sees in some quarters where Kierkegaard is held up as a champion of the *philosophia perennis*. We are told by authors such as Dr. Heinemann that the great value of Kierkegaard for our time is that he and the other existentialist philosophers show us a way of doing philosophy that frees us from the narrow bigotry of analysts. Dr. Heinemann is by no means uncritical in his enthusiasm for existentialism, and his very careful estimate of its significance is quite different from the crude view described above. Yet even

Dr. Heinemann is emphatic in his opinion that Kierkegaard's importance lies in his opposition to such a philosophy as what he calls ' Logical Positivism '. So he hails Kierkegaard as one who can free us from the prison of our contemporary philosophy. Here Dr. Heinemann's point is essentially the same as the other. The error of this view is that it makes an anachronistic opponent of analysis out of one who never knew anything about the technique, and one could with equal justice say that Locke, the father of empiricism, was really an opponent of linguistic analysis, the twentieth century empiricism. It may be asked whether our proposal has not been an equally anachronistic interpretation but this is to miss the point that we are only using a technique to disentangle Kierkegaard's points from their century-old expression ; whereas the view we criticise would regard Kierkegaard as presenting a philosophy which opposes the philosophical technique developed in the century following his death. A philosophy is not like a scientific theory and is never disproved. We can kill a scientific theory but a philosophy dies of old age. There is life in these dry bones that we see in Kierkegaard because he has grasped essential points about religious faith. If these points are indeed essential then they must be expressed in terms of the contemporary linguistic method.

(i) *Faith is not proof.*

The first point that Kierkegaard makes is that religious faith can in no sense be described as proof. Of course, the word ' proof ' has a variety of meanings, as may be seen from the following examples.

> (a) ' The counsel for the prosecution brought forward proof of the defendant's guilt.'
> (b) ' The proof of Archimedes' Principle is easily shown.'
> (c) ' The proof of Pythagoras' theorem always baffled me.'

In (a) the prosecution has been said to prove the man's guilt. What does proof amount to here? It is the description of all the known facts of the situation which show that the defendant either was seen by reliable witnesses as he committed the crime or else could have committed it, and his other actions are such as remove any reasonable doubt that he committed the crime. In the court

of law, then, the proof which is required is history, the recon-
struction of a situation by means of tested evidence. We bring
forward one piece of evidence after the other until we have enough
to remove any doubt as to what should be the verdict. This is
what we usually mean. But there is another type of legal proof
which has nothing to do with evidence. This is the situation,
where both counsel are agreed about the facts, but the defence
asks ' Is it libel? ' or ' Was there neglect? ' Now, it is the context
in which the question is asked rather than the form of these words
that makes them peculiar. Prof. Wisdom says :

> ' In courts of law there often arise questions which it
> is difficult to settle although the " material " facts are known
> and agreed upon. For example, counsel for the plaintiff
> argues that there has been negligence, counsel for the defen-
> dant that there has not. Before the argument begins, it is
> already agreed, perhaps, that the plaintiff found a snail in
> the bottle of ginger-beer and that this beer was bottled by
> the defendant, though not sold by him and so on.'[1]

Prof. Wisdom quotes Mr. Glanville Williams's description of these
questions as questions of words. This is a very paradoxical statement, and Prof. Wisdom examines it carefully to show how it can
be very misleading even though it is true. It is misleading because
if the questions the court was trying to settle were questions of
words, would not the discussion as to whether they are or not
also be a matter of words? Thus Mr. Williams would not wish
to say his argument is not designed to make people alter their
verbal habits but to deliver them from a misleading idea as to
the nature of legal discussion. We remember that the question
' Was it negligence? ' could be asked before he knew that there
was a snail in the bottle of ginger-beer and also after he has heard
all the evidence. Now it is possible that the question could be
settled by means of the evidence. Then we would say that the
question is a question of fact. Shall we then say that Mr. Williams
is right in calling the other question a question of words? He
is right in so far as he points out that we are not asking for any
more evidence in order to complete our picture. This is an
extremely important point which must be grasped if we are to

[1] Wisdom, op. cit., p. 249.

understand what legal inquiry is. Wisdom says that our inability to decide the issue after getting the evidence may make us feel that the inquiry has been a failure ' in the way an inquiry as to what is happening behind a curtain is a failure when the evidences this side of the curtain do not enable us to decide what is happening behind it '.[1] This is a muddle because we know what has happened, and whether reflection has produced an answer or not it has enabled us to understand the case better. We see how close and how far this case is from those where we would and others where we would not speak of negligence. But Mr. Williams's suggestion is misleading because it makes us think of legal discussion in terms of an equally wrong model suggested by ' question of words '. It is not words that are in debate but the defendant's guilt. We may insist that the court is concerned to find out whether there was negligence.

Legal proof then is establishing that a person has done something by (*a*) direct evidence or (*b*) indirect evidence (' circumstantial ') which is enough to remove any ' reasonable doubt ' or (*c*) by showing that the facts which are not in dispute are such that the case is of such and such a legal character (e.g. negligence).

In our second example we have the scientific use of the word ' proof '. The proof of Archimedes' principle is something with which we are all familiar whether we try an experiment or simply recall the story about its discovery. We place a body in water and we notice that the water rises. We measure the volume of water and find that the volume of water displaced is equivalent to the volume of the body we placed in the water. This experiment is repeated with different bodies and in each case we find the result is the same. Therefore we see that we have ' proved ' that the Principle of Archimedes is true.

A scientific proof consists of a method of verifying a theory or hypothesis. We start off from the observation of certain unfamiliar aspects of a familiar situation. Thus we noticed that the bath which was half-full is now almost three-quarters full. This gives rise to the question ' Is the bath half-full or three-quarters full? '. We remove the body and we see that the bath is (as we would say) really only half-full. So we suggest that the body in the water makes the water rise. This explanation

[1] Wisdom, op. cit., p. 251.

' accounts for ' the unfamiliar phenomenon. The next step is not simply to account for the past but to make trial predictions from our theory using the methods of deductive logic and of mathematics. As long as these predictions are confirmed by our experience, we retain the theory. If our expectation turns out not to be true then we abandon the theory or at least modify it. However, this is not all. Even if all has gone well so far, we shall not be satisfied, and we keep on predicting and checking. We shall test the predictive power or reliability of our theory first within the original field of experience, later changing the condition so as to pass beyond it. The next stage is that of making predictions within a field of experience which is covered by another theory. Here there are a number of possible results. We may find that the two theories conflict and one is inferior to the other : if so, we change the inferior theory to make it fit with the other. Another possibility is that they should lead to the same predictions. If this is the case and no changes are necessary in our calculus we shall say that the two theories are fundamentally the same. If the calculi and the concepts are quite dissimilar then we shall choose the simpler calculus. We see then that the main elements in scientific proof are (*a*) predictability, (*b*) coherence and (*c*) simplicity.

We come now to our last example. Pythagoras' theorem or any other theorem in Euclidean geometry is proved to be true by a process of strict deductive reasoning. We sometimes distinguish this sense of ' proof' from others by calling it a demonstration. Thus when someone says that he does not understand the theorem of Pythagoras or does not ' see ' it we do not take him to mean that there is anything wrong with the proof. It is true that Euclid's first proposition cannot be established by means of the axioms, but this only shows that Euclid's system is not rigorous enough. His deduction was not logical, and though he might make it *obvious* the proposition was not *demonstrated*. In constructing a system of Mathematics then we do not ask if something can be seen to be true but rather ask if the proposition follows from the axioms and the definitions alone. It is quite irrelevant whether someone is convinced or not. In our example A says to B, ' The proof of Pythagoras' theorem always baffled me '. If B knows the proof he may undertake to demonstrate the theorem to A. Now, there is no question here of the theorem not being proved already. Moreover, it is assumed that A can be made to understand the theorem's proof if the steps are shown to him carefully and the whole thing explained. Pure mathematics is in fact reducible to logic—that is, it is a completely logical structure. A branch of mathematics is a set of propositions capable of abstract formulation in such a way that every proposition can be demonstrated to follow from the primitive concepts and the primitive propositions.

When we say with Kierkegaard that faith is not proof we see that we are saying much more than might be thought. We are saying that religious faith is unlike (*a*) the method of the lawyer who seeks to establish something, (*b*) the method of the scientist who wants to discover something, (*c*) the method of the mathematician who seeks to construct a system that will be true. How is faith different from these three processes of thought? It is easiest to start with the last. Any attempt to prove God's existence *a priori* is bound to fail because of three things. The first is that such a proof is a demonstration and not a persuasion resulting in conviction. Faith is the way in which we become convinced that God does exist. In other words, it is not a demonstration of the truth of a system of abstract propositions. It would be quite nonsensical to say that we demonstrate God's existence when we believe in Him. It would be like saying that I demonstrate to myself the truth of the proposition that my wife loves me or that my mother has faith in me. The second reason why it is said that *a priori* proof of God is bound to fail is the purely logical point that existential statements in fact cannot be proved. We dealt with this in an earlier chapter and for the moment we need say no more about it. The final reason is that in the case of faith there can be no such certainty about its belief as there must be in the case of demonstration. Let us now look at the second example of the use of the word 'proof'. Is faith at all like a scientific proof? Sir Henry Jones, in the once-famous *A Faith that Enquires*, claims for religious faith the same sort of status as a scientific hypothesis :

'It is for this reason that I call religious faith the supreme hypothesis, because religion bears upon the whole destiny

of man and of all that he values, as does the scientific hypothesis upon all that comes within the borders of the science.
There is nothing real except in virtue of it, nothing intelligible except in its light. If the hypothesis breaks down,
nothing remains except unintelligible, chaotic particulars '.[1]

We have seen that Sir Henry's anxiety to give religion as important a place in the field of knowledge as science led him astray.
In an earlier chapter we saw that faith was not to be described
as a hypothesis. Though none can doubt the strength and sin-
cerity of Henry Jones's faith it is very doubtful whether his
description does justice to that very faith. It is surely a misguided
zeal which makes him and so many theologians commend religion
as being every bit as sound as science because after all science is
not absolutely objective, not really proved and so on.

> ' But, surely, it will be said, the religious hypothesis is
> . . . the most insecure as well as the most daring of all
> constructive conceptions. . . . No hypothesis, as a hypothesis,
> can ever be finally proved ; human knowledge is never
> complete. . . .
> What shall we say to these objections? Both are valid :
> within their own region, they can be urged in the same way
> against all hypotheses, even those of Mathematics. No
> hypothesis is completely worked out.'[2]

The whole point of his argument now seems to be an attack on
the very criterion he had used to measure faith. Faith was the
best hypothesis, but now we are told that a hypothesis is not as
intellectually respectable as people imagine. This is to obliterate
the essential differences which are brought out in our discussion
of Kierkegaard's concept of the leap. Kierkegaard's refusal to
say that faith was as good as or like scientific proof is important
in that it points to these differences. Faith is not an explanation
which enables us to predict anything.

The final example is the legal use of ' proof '. This is clearly
not relevant to faith. The religious man is not concerned to make
any judgment about the relation of anyone to a set of facts or
again about the way in which these facts are to be described.

[1] Henry Jones, op. cit., p. 93.   [2] ibid., pp. 99–100.

But here as in the scientific example we may feel that there is something which is relevant to the philosophy of religion and to theology. This we shall discuss later. Here it is necessary only to point out how unnatural it is to imagine the believer going through a process of argument such as the lawyer uses to prove that so-and-so is guilty or innocent. He no more proves God than he does himself. The process of reasoning through which he goes when he makes this move is not such that one can either say that he is proving anything or that his argument could be made a proof.

(ii) *The rebuttal of Rationalism.*

This point now brings us to the second fruitful contribution of Kierkegaard. Historically Kierkegaard was important as a critic of Hegel. We have seen that he did in fact demolish the Hegelian philosophy of religion. After Kierkegaard Hegel was out of date, because he pointed out the error of the basic idea in Hegel's system which is the identity of thought and reality or existence. This is of immense significance for us as we do philosophy of religion in our day, because it is time to say that this border-line country between philosophy and theology has been the happy hunting ground of those who have never been cured of Hegelianism. It is thus helpful to bring out Kierkegaard's point more clearly by comparing it with the work of Moore and Wisdom. First, however, let us look at one or two contemporary writers, and by means of some quotations of their work we shall see that philosophy of religion to-day is hardly less 'systematic' than Hegel was. Prof. Hodgson wrote an important book some years ago in which he sought to describe his own understanding of philosophical theology. Whether *Towards a Christian Philosophy* represents Dr. Hodgson's views now or not we cannot say, and indeed is not relevant to our discussion. For we are not concerned to criticise Hodgson's work, but simply to use it as an example of the significant work on Philosophy of Religion done in our century. In the book mentioned Hodgson says that philosophy has two main characteristics :

' (1) It is an attempt to understand the why and wherefore of things in which the philosopher explores more thoroughly and systematically the plain man's question : (2) it inevitably becomes an attempt to find the key to unlock the secret of the unified system of reality, that secret which in principle contains the explanation of *everything*, since to explain anything is to show how it fits into an intelligible system of which it is a part.'[1]

Now Hegel's programme was almost exactly this. He too wanted to explain to John Smith what he really meant and to explore more fully than the ordinary man could the extreme reaches of his questions. Then the second element which Prof. Hodgson describes could be taken as a description of what Hegel tried to do in his System. The late Prof. John Laird has much the same thing to say in his first series of Gifford Lectures.[2]

> ' I am asserting that philosophy, philosophical theology and metaphysics, as I interpret these studies, are not a kind of poetry. I do not say that they are sciences in every sense of that hospitable term. They may not all be of the purest analytical water or meticulously experimental, but they are on the side of *scientia* in the general sense that they profess to be based upon reasoned argument. . . . We are still asking whether a reasoned enquiry into the nature of things is evidence of the deformity of reality. We still want to know whether . . . we can build on a solid foundation of rational argument.'[3]

Prof. Laird's quest is another way of seeking that explanation of all things which was Hegel's aim. For Laird, as for Hegel, the task of the philosopher of religion is to sit in judgment on the deliverances of the religious life. The philosopher says ' You tell me that you believe in God and His providence. Very well! Now let us see whether these things are really true or not '. Hegel had been emphatic from the start that the only judge of all issues was philosophy. Do we not hear an echo of this enchantment in the words of our old text book—Galloway's *Philosophy of Religion* ?

---

[1] Hodgson, *Towards a Christian Philosophy*, London, Nisbet, 1943, p. 19.
[2] Laird, *Theism and Cosmology*, London, Allen and Unwin, 1940.
[3] ibid., p. 33.

' One might say . . . that religion itself imposes on us the obligation of trying to justify it by philosophical thought. . . . A Philosophy of Religion then, if it is true to its taste and frankly faces the issues it has raised, cannot avoid dealing with the problem of the ultimate truth of religion. . . . A justification can only be given, if it is to be given at all, by speculative thought'[1]

It is just this assumption, that the only justification of religion which is possible is the sort of justification which the speculative philosopher gives, which Kierkegaard protested against so strongly. In the interest of philosophy itself as well as that of honest religion he wanted people to realise that religion was first and last a matter of what people do. It is utterly fantastic to imagine that the religious man must await the philosopher's decision before he can believe. The whole point is that he does believe and will go on believing whatever the philosopher says to him. Moreover, says Kierkegaard, by what authority does the philosopher claim the task of judging religion?

It is interesting to compare this with Prof. Wisdom's description of the great relief which he experienced on reading Moore.

' In the preface to his *Principia Ethica* Moore wrote " It appears to me that in Ethics, as in all other philosophical studies, the difficulties and disagreements of which its history is full, are mainly due to a very simple cause : namely to the attempt to answer questions, without first discovering precisely *what* question it is which you desire to answer? "

I remember with what renewed hope I read these words. I was beginning the study of philosophy . . . and there had grown in me the unspoken fear that I should never understand the stuff. Here, in Moore, was someone first-rate suggesting that philosophers themselves do not know very well what they are talking about.'[2]

It is the same sort of relief and renewed hope which Kierkegaard gives us, though one often wishes he were half as simple and direct as Moore. When we flounder in the sea of confusion which confronts us, as theologians are considering their subject

[1] Galloway, *The Philosophy of Religion*, Clark, Edinburgh, 1914, pp. 33-4.
[2] Wisdom, op. cit., p. 120.

philosophically, it is salutary to be reminded by a brilliant thinker like Kierkegaard that the metaphysical theologians have not paused to ask what questions they have to decide. Thus in dealing with religion the philosopher has been wont to ask ' What corner of Reality can you occupy? '. Then begins the endless discussion of whether God is a part of Reality or in fact the Absolute. And Kierkegaard reminds us that all this is a fantastic game with abstract concepts which have very little to do with the concretions we had in the beginning. Even more relevant is the technique which Moore employs which is that of changing the question ' Do we know these things? ' into the question ' What is the analysis of what we know in knowing these things? ' Wisdom says that this move bothers people—' they feel that they came to buy one thing and that the man behind the counter is trying to sell them something just as good—better in fact '. It is not that Moore never asks ' How do we know? ' but that this never leads him to ask ' Do we know? '. This is puzzling and disappointing because of the lingering idea that philosophy is science, a higher sort of science. Kierkegaard's rejection of the Hegelian identification of essential religion with reason or metaphysics brings us, I believe, to a similar realisation. The slogan that ' subjectivity is truth ' is thus valuable as showing that the philosophy of religion must move away from the old notion of philosophy as giving a picture of Reality.

The two points which we have tried to bring out here are then these. (1) It is wrong to think of religion as being a crude form of reasoning for any conclusion. We have seen that faith is not proof. If this means anything it means that the rationalist interpretation of faith as being essentially reason is wrong and the theologians who are so anxious to show how rational a thing is are misguided. Kierkegaard gives a very full meaning to Pascal's epigram—' Le coeur a ses raisons que la raison ne connait pas '. (2) It is equally an error to think that the philosophy of religion should ' justify ' the religious position. Kierkegaard's repudiation of the philosopher's dangerous help is shown to be a most sensible action by the contribution of the Cambridge analysts to our understanding of philosophy. We see that philosophy is not a science and that it no more makes religion plausible than it makes the existence of the external world plausible. ' Plausible ' is a word that has no place in the language of philosophy of religion.

(iii) *The rebuttal of the empirical error.*

There is another kind of error which Kierkegaard was concerned to avoid and expose. Not only was he opposed to the rationalist philosopher whose reduction of religion to reason distorted faith beyond recognition but he contended that the empirical approach exemplified by Schleiermacher was no better. The too empirical approach of a great deal of Protestant theology with its stress on 'Experience' was as repugnant to him as Hegel's too rational approach. There has been some doubt about his attitude towards mysticism, and some people have felt it odd to deny that such an intensely pious and zealous Christian was a mystic. Yet Kierkegaard in fact left us in no doubt about his attitude. We recall that Martensen was profoundly influenced by mysticism and it is safe to suggest that Kierkegaard was familiar with the contention that mysticism was true or 'pure religion' (the phrase is Dean Inge's). This gives greater point to his condemnation of mysticism. For him the mystic was too impatient, unwilling to wait for God's self-revelation and thus intent on 'taking the Kingdom of Heaven by force' whereas the process is really a slow one.[1] The later scandal about Adler led him to make a study of the problem of mysticism which he intended discussing in the *Book on Adler*, a book that was never published. Adler was a parish priest in Bornholm, and in 1843 he published a volume of sermons which, he claimed, were written under the direct guidance of the grace of the Lord Jesus. He says in the preface that one night in December of the previous year he had received a revelation of Christ Himself. Christ had commanded him to rise from his bed and write certain things and also to burn the work he had done on Hegel's philosophy. The upshot of the matter was that he was dismissed from his living and pensioned off in 1845. However, he published an account of the whole affair—the revelation, his examination by his superior clergy and also some works on theology. The whole affair seems to have interested Kierkegaard enormously; and amongst the other obvious reasons such as the irony of the situa-

[1] Cp. *Journals*, 61.

L

tion[1] it is undeniable that there was the reason that it raised the question of the relation of faith to certain experiences. And whilst he would be the last to say that faith has no relation at all to feelings yet he was not content with the way in which theologians sometimes talked of faith as being nothing more than feeling.

The classical exponent of the romantic theology was Schleiermacher (1768–1834) whose famous 'Addresses on Religion to its Cultural Despisers' gave powerful expression to this type of theology. Throughout the book he is speaking to those intellectuals of his time who regarded Christianity as being scarcely worth the trouble of disproof. Schleiermacher felt that men must be made aware of religion as something to be enjoyed and not as something to be analysed. Religion was an experience and not another name for either metaphysics or morals. There is nothing in this to which anyone can take exception. However, the way in which Schleiermacher understood this apparently innocuous thesis was novel and startling. The seat of religion, he contends, is not in reason or conscience or will. Religion is the direct contact of the soul with God ; and if it has this directness then it must have its source in *feeling*. 'Pious contemplation is the immediate consciousness of the universal existence of all things in and through the Infinite, and of all temporal things in and through the Eternal.' It is well known that Schleiermacher had emphasised the place of intuition together with feeling in the first edition of the *Addresses* whilst later he talked of religion simply as feeling. H. R. Mackintosh makes a very careful estimate of Schleiermacher's argument and gives it as his verdict that while he most probably intended that ' feeling ' should mean a mode of apprehension his argument often proceeds on the psychological sense and would have broken down were it not for the ambiguity. ' In short, he exemplifies a well known logical fallacy by arguing that since religion is not mere knowledge we are entitled to deny that it is a whole in which knowledge is a constitutive element.'

An entry in the *Journal* of 1849 makes the same point as Kierkegaard made earlier, that this type of theology is just the same sort of distortion of faith as Hegelianism. He had said that what both Hegel and Schleiermacher call faith is really nothing

---

[1] A chapter of the *Book* was to deal with Adler ' as a satire on the Hegelian philosophy and on the Present Day '.

more than the ' spiritual atmosphere we breathe '. In 1849 he says, that the aberration of his time is ' that faith has been made into something so inward that it disappears completely in the end '.[1] This had two strands of meaning for Kierkegaard which might be described as the moral and the epistemological. The moral meaning of this remark is that if faith is simply a matter of having certain experiences then it never does anything. And ' faith without works is dead '. This was something that Kierkegaard never doubted but did however feel more strongly towards the end of his life. In *Fear and Trembling* he says that there is nothing to distinguish the knight of faith from someone else. Later he felt that this was saying too much, and that there were certain ordinary situations which would be such that the Christian could not take part in them. However, it is the epistemological point which concerns us here. This can be stated briefly thus : faith, when it is made synonymous with feeling, is in danger of becoming dissolved into nothing. It is in fact a reduction of faith. Let us first consider the direct knowledge which the feeling of absolute dependence gave us according to Schleiermacher. We can interpret this as asserting ' I know God exists because I have a direct experience of Him '. We might even substitute the word ' feeling ' for ' experience ' and rewrite the sentence thus ' I feel that God does exist and so I am certain that God's existence is real (or that it is true that God exists)'. This type of statement is of very little use, because as it stands it is only an empty tautology—that is, a tautology which does not illumine anything, has no meaning even as a tautology. If it is true that I have a direct experience of God then God must exist. The difficulty, however, is to see whether saying ' I feel that God exists ' or ' I have direct experience of God ' is the same as saying ' I know that God exists '. To revert to Schleiermacher, if he says that he knows God exists because he has a feeling of absolute dependence this is wrong. ' I feel absolutely dependent ' is indeed a very peculiar assertion and one which if given an ample enough background might indeed be said to be a religious assertion. However, it is no *reason* or evidence. Therefore however strange the statement may be it implies nothing other than an as yet undescribed state of mind or emotional situation. No matter

[1] *Papirer* X[2] A.207.

how we choose to put this 'experience' argument it is always open to this objection. It must always avoid becoming something definite and so always remains something nebulous. We can say that it is unique, but this proves nothing about its logical character. It only shows, in fact, something which can be true of almost any statement. Consider the statement ' You don't know what a holiday is until you've been to Butlin's '. Let us assume that one of our friends has made this statement and we, anxious to cultivate his taste and so on, seek to free him of this strange delusion. ' You've been to Torquay, haven't you? ' we say. ' Oh yes ' he says ' but it's not like Butlin's. That was no holiday '. Paris, New York, Miami—no matter where, there is no place that he has been which is good enough. In this way he has proved that a holiday at Butlin's is unique. In other words, he has made the statement analytic—a holiday is a holiday at Butlin's. Yet it is clear that if his wife takes him to the Edinburgh Festival instead of Butlin's he may come to say that it was better than Butlin's. That is, he has not told us anything about this holiday by saying that it was unique. The characteristic of a holiday which makes it unique is nothing other than its being one in Butlin's. The fact that he changes his mind precludes the possibility of this being an idea for which he will live and die.

By saying that religious faith is feeling this way or that way we are like the man who says ' I can feel there's water in the ground ' or ' I can feel there's gold in that mountain '. Now if we ask him why he is so sure, he may reply that just as we learn that there is water or gold by digging so he can tell by a certain feeling that there is water and that it is at such and such a depth. The story may go on for a long time but in the end all that the man establishes is that ' there is water five foot below the ground ' means for him ' I have certain sensations in my hand and arm '. Then he is no longer using the first statement in the way in which he was first assumed to be (or indeed perhaps the way in which he claimed he was) using it. That is, he is not really telling us anything about the existence of water at this depth. In the same way, if we say that what faith consists of is feeling then we shall also be found to say that when we say ' I have faith in God ' or ' I have faith that there is a Providence whose grace sustains me ', all we are saying is that this is our feeling. Thus we are not saying anything about God at all and saying nothing about the sustaining grace either. We see that this does indeed make faith disappear. On this analysis religious statements are made quite the reverse of what they are. Kierkegaard insisted that faith is a real relation to God in the same way as an assertion about physical objects or people is an assertion about my relation to something other than myself. He felt that people were so ' busy about getting a truer and truer conception of God ' that they had forgotten ' the very first step, that one should fear God '.[1] Worship is a relation to God.[2]

This was no academic or unreal issue for Kierkegaard and he was contending against real opponents not imaginary ones. Martensen had been saying that knowledge must start from immediate perception of its object and that it is thus compelled to receive the light of truth as a gift humbly and trustingly. ' The assertion of Christians, that faith is the mother of knowledge, is substantially confirmed by the analogy of all other spheres of human knowledge ; for all human knowledge has its root in an immediate perception of the object. And as it is useless for one who lacks hearing to talk about music, as it is useless for one who has no sense of colours, to develop a theory of colour, the same holds true respecting the conjunction of sacred things.'[3] This is the same sort of fallacy as we have been discussing. The only point that is established is that one has certain experiences the other person is not having. And whether he has these experiences or not is not to the point when we ask what reason he has for saying that God exists. In other words, the importance of these feelings has nothing to do with the objectivity claim ot religious statements and to emphasise them is to argue against objectivity. Now just as this was no academic issue for Kierkegaard so for us the matter is a live problem. Ever since William James published his *Varieties of Religious Experience* the bearing of psychology on religion has been in the front rank of intellectual interest. The title of Freud's work, *The Future of an Illusion*, is as it were a summary of the attitude of many psychologists, philosophers and laymen towards religious faith. The kindest attitude will not say as much as we want said. Conclusions are

---

[1] *Postscript*, p. 391.   [2] ibid. p. 369.
[3] Martensen, *Christian Dogmatics*, p. 59.

reached by the psychologist about the illusory character of religous faith and are put forward as ' scientific truths '. What the theologian usually does is to reply that the psychologist is too pretentious and is really going beyond the limits of his field. It is no part of the scientist's task, it is claimed, to give ' final explanations ' which can be provided only by philosophy and theology. We have already seen that behind this attitude and answer lies the old idea which dies very hard indeed that the philosopher and the theologian are super-scientists. They receive the conclusions and the achievements of the scientist, and then start their work of criticism and unification. This is a most misleading picture of the work of the philosopher and the theologian ; and even were it true these two would then be fighting for the final claim to the spoils. Now our answer to the psychologist must be quite different from this. What answer can we give? First, we can ask him whether he has given us a complete account of the psychological processes. Then we can ask him what he means to claim by saying that religious faith is an illusion. Is he saying that the psychological processes are the same in both cases? They may or may not be, but the essential point is that this says nothing about the logical character of the religious man's statements. And it is this which interests us as philosophers and theologians. Here is the kernel of truth in the old view of the function of these purely reflective studies as against that of science. So if the claim that religion is an illusion is to be upheld it must be shown that the religious man's assertions are capable of being shown to be false in the same way as it can be shown that a man who has an illusion of seeing a dagger is making a false statement when he says ' I see a dagger before me '. Unless the man's mind is deranged he can be brought to confess that he only ' thought ' this, or that it only ' seemed ' to him that there was a dagger. ' I felt that I saw a dagger '. In other words, the statement can never be dissociated from an assertion about himself so that its truth is that of an autobiographical assertion. We have seen that religious statements cannot be reduced to statements about feeling. To do this is to leave out of our account an essential feature of these statements which may be described as their ' reality interest ' or objective character. I do worship God and know Him.

(iv) *Religious faith is the answer to a limiting question.*[1]

From our discussion we learn two things—(i) that the logic of religous statements is very complex, (ii) that faith is essentially objective in the sense that it is not identifiable with psychological statements. Kierkegaard's insistence on this second point leads us to ask for a description of faith's objectivity. One point is perfectly clear—we shall not be able to give an extensive definition of the objective constituent of the situation. Neither shall we be able to give any sort of literal description of it in the way in which the speculative philosopher seems to tell us what goes on in the mind of God. All this is what Kierkegaard ridiculed in the *Postscript* when he showed that the assumption underlying the Hegelian system was that the philosopher could view things in the same way as God. However, this is not the only sort of objectivity that we can have. There is also the objectivity which characterises ethical statements.

We cannot discuss the character of ethical statements at any length, but we shall try to see how it is true to say that they are rational or objective. To do this we must consider an example of ethical discourse. Black and White are two friends indulging in some gossip about Smith. Black says ' I always thought Smith was an irreproachable character, but I must say that his behaviour of late has made me think otherwise '.

' What? ' asks White ' What has he done? '.

Black : ' Haven't you heard about the brutal way in which he fired that young man from his office? '

White : ' Oh that! '

Black : ' What do you mean " Oh that! "? I should have thought that sacking a young chap who's just married and setting up home would be enough to warrant anyone calling him a blackguard.'

White : ' But really, there's more to it than just that, you know. That boy had been causing trouble for ages and had actually stolen money at least twice.'

Black : ' I'm not convinced.'

White : ' I know it is true because it was the Head Cashier

---

[1] The term ' limiting question ' is borrowed from Mr. Stephen Toulmin's *Reason in Ethics*, Cambridge University Press, 1950. In this section in particular I am very much indebted to this book.

who told me. He had been wanting to sack the fellow from the first but Smith wouldn't hear of it. He wanted to give him a chance because he was a married man.'

Black : ' Well that changes things completely. I was puzzled and wasn't really sure that it was true. If what you say is true—and I'm not doubting it, mind—then Smith is really what I thought he was, after all.'

Now the various kinds of subjective theories of ethics attempt an analysis of ethical concepts in terms of the attitudes of the speaker and the hearer. The most celebrated contemporary exponent of this view is C. L. Stevenson. Stevenson's analysis is an attempt to put forward a subjective theory which is free from the deficiencies which vitiate the straightforward theories. He admits that to say ' this is good ' is not the same as saying ' I like this '—they cannot be simply equated. It is nevertheless a fact that different people use different tests in coming to a decision so that one person will say that meekness is good and another that it is bad. Stevenson's contention is that ethical disagreement is disagreement in attitude and not disagreement in belief. This is the way in which he explains the disagreement which may occur when people know all the facts. Disagreement in belief is a disagreement about a statement which can be revised in the light of more information. Thus I may say that it is too late to plant Brussels sprouts in July and someone else will disagree. This disagreement can be removed as we would say by ' proof '. The other kind of disagreement is an opposition of preferences, desires, etc.,—e.g. I say ' I think a Martini is the best possible appetiser ' and my friend replied ' I disagree. There is nothing better than a good Amontillado '. Stevenson goes on to analyse ' This is good ' in terms of two kinds of meaning : descriptive and emotive. The component of meaning refers to a fact which can be verified while the second aims at persuading the hearer to behave in some way or other. The model Stevenson suggests for ' This is good ' consists of the conjunction of (*a*) ' I approve of this ' and (*b*) ' Do so as well '.[1]

Despite the subtlety of Stevenson's analysis, however, the theory has one fatal weakness which we can see if we consider our example. In the course of the discussion White could be

[1] Cp. C. L. Stevenson, *Ethics and Language*, New Haven, 1944, p. 26.

said with some truth to be intent on changing Black's attitude. This is a very important aspect of ethical terms and we shall have cause to return to this later. The point at the moment is that White was not simply trying to change Black's attitude : he was also giving him a reason which he claimed was sufficient ground for believing that his attitude was wrong. In other words, he was giving him the factual premiss from which he was to draw his ethical conclusion. Now, if the account of ethics which Stevenson gives us is correct then he must deny that there is any sense in which the reason we have mentioned was a reason at all. The question of the validity of the inference from the factual premiss is ' devoid of interest '. And this is surely a most paradoxical statement to make. For if it were devoid of interest why does Black admit that the premiss *does* in fact change the whole situation? The theory seems very attractive because it carries with it a suggestion that this is strict science but in fact the philosopher is not interested in the scientific matters involved. What he is trying to do is to prescribe a new usage for ethical words, and to legislate as to what they should mean. We see, then, that questions of ethics, like questions of logic, are concerned, not with subjective relations—that is, with what is ' attractive ' (to-me or to-you) or with what ' seems right ' (again to -A or to -B) but with objective concepts. The description of these concepts is an intricate matter ; but that there are such concepts forming a *terminus ad quem* of ethical argument is now clear.

Such an analysis as this enables us to see the outlines of a theory of ethical objectivity and by analogy that of the objectivity of religious assertions. We have no difficulty in seeing that they too, like questions of ethics, are not concerned with subjective relations. Thus despite the apparent similarity between the man looking at the sunset who says ' Haven't felt so much at home, no sir, not since I left California ' and the believer who humbly says ' Holy, Holy, Holy, Lord God of hosts, heaven and earth are full of thy glory ' the difference between them is great. The first statement is almost entirely a matter of attitude whereas the second is not. The story which the first tells is that of nostalgia when the beautiful red sunset like the proverbially glorious sun of California induces not only a longing memory but a strange sense of being there already. But all this is a story about our American friend's feelings and he would perhaps express it in very homely telling language. 'That's the way things look to me. And after all, I'm telling you about my own opinions and my own feelings, aren't I?'. It could not be better expressed. However, the saint, sophisticated or simple, will never be content with this. We may trick him into saying this. So the agnostic will say to him that he just cannot pray, and he sees no sense in praying. To which the saint replies that there is great sense in it if he but tries. 'When I pray' he says 'I feel that I am being changed and being re-created. A new sense of vocation and a new courage, a new urgency and a new peace—these are the things prayer gives me'. 'Ah' says the agnostic 'I see what you mean. This is the sense there is in it. It is a psychological device to get these feelings'. This the saint will deny very definitely, and he will then say 'What is important is that God is there'. And it is this reference to a concept which is meant to be the end-point of the discussion which makes faith so much like ethics.

Having reached this concept the argument usually stops. Thus if I say that we ought to have done something, there may be a certain amount of discussion until we reach the point when I say 'Because such-and-such is right'. However, when this answer is given the discussion about the course of action is at an end—unless the questioner happens to be a metaphysician. If he is he will then go on to ask another question, 'Why ought I to do what is right?' It is this kind of question which is most like the question 'Does God exist?'. And it is just this compari-son which we can make on the basis of Kierkegaard's work. In Chapter III of *Philosophical Fragments* which deals with 'the absolute paradox' Kierkegaard talks of the paradoxical passion of reason and the paradoxical consequence to which it leads. On first reading one is inclined to dismiss this as being a purely literary piece of writing whose only philosophical point is that it makes a neat introduction to an argument which could well do without it. I must confess that I had always been inclined to view it thus until recently. The usefulness of this strange talk is again seen only if we apply the technique of linguistic analysis. The usefulness is that it shows how similar the religious question is to that peculiar sort of question we sometimes have if we drive an ethical discussion beyond the point where we bring forward our ethical concept. Let us look at this argument of Kierkegaard's more closely. It is very brief and must be considered very carefully. He begins by saying that Socrates, the life-long student of human nature, had not ' been able to make up his mind whether he was a stranger monster than Typhon, or a mixture of a gentler and simpler sort, partaking of something divine '.[1] The paradoxical appearance of this statement, Kierkegaard insists, is nothing to its discredit ; ' for the paradox is the source of the thinker's passion, and the thinker without a paradox is like a lover without feeling, a paltry mediocrity '.[2] It had occurred to Kierkegaard before that the great thinker, the true philosopher, was not the person who had constructed a system which would explain everything but rather he who recognised that above every such system there was a paradox.[3] The philosopher is always trying to express something that cannot be expressed. This is what lends his thinking the passion that Kierkegaard tells of. He points out that this is characteristic of the ordinary individual as well as the philosopher *in so far as* ' in thinking he participates in something transcending himself '. This remark is very enlightening and fruitful. Here Kierkegaard has put his finger on the very thing that makes our thinking so important for us—the consciousness that it is the means whereby we can reach to what transcends us. So there is in thought a certain drive or momentum, an obstinacy, even a thrill which makes us want to carry it on and on—we do not know the end of the quest, we only know the way. This uncertainty indicates the possibility that this road may prove the destruction of Reason itself. ' The highest pitch of every passion is always to will its own downfall ; and so it is also the supreme of the Reason to seek a collision, though this collision must in one way or another prove its undoing. The supreme paradox of all thought is to discover that which thought cannot think.[4] Now, what would such a collision and self-destruction be? It is well known that Bertrand Russell illustrated how it is possible in logic to be carried to a paradox by the very rules of logic, so that in a calculus we reach an impossible formula. This is an example of the way in which thinking

[1] *Philosophical Fragments*, p. 29. The reference is to *Phaedrus*, 229E.
[2] loc. cit.
[3] Cp. *Papirer*, II, A.439. [4] loc. cit.

can bring us to the point where we seem to contradict the very rationality that made us make the move. We can take the Russellian paradox as our first example. This is the paradox of asserting ' This sentence is false '. The paradox is that if we assert it then we are saying that it is true whereas the plain meaning of the sentence is that it is false. If the sentence is false we can denote it by the symbol $\sim p$. But the sentence or proposition can itself only be described or denoted by the symbol P. Therefore if we are denying P what we are saying is $\sim P$. Therefore $\sim P \equiv \sim (\sim p)$ and so p is true. But how can we say that p is true when the original proposition was that p is false? However, this kind of paradox is not very instructive, and in fact it depends on a wrong assumption as to the logical nature of propositions. That is, it can only be true if propositions can refer to themselves. The term ' This sentence ' is in fact meaningless as used in the example we quoted, because there is no sentence given apart from the one asserted of which the term is a part. A much more interesting example for our purpose is the metaphysician in the ethical discussion who wanted to know why anyone should do what is right. In his argument Kierkegaard maintains that Socrates was doubtful about his own nature because he was aware of something he did not know. Even if we begin by assuming that we know what man is we shall reach the same impasse as Socrates.

' So then we know what man is, and this wisdom . . . may progressively grow richer and more significant, and with it also the Truth. But now the Reason hesitates . . . ; for the paradoxical passion of the Reason is aroused and seeks a collision ; without rightly understanding itself it is bent upon its own downfall. This is like what happens in connection with the paradox of love. Man lives undisturbed a self-centred life, until there awakens in him the paradox of self-love, in the form of love for another, the object of his longing ——. The lover is so completely transformed that he scarcely recognises himself. . . . In like manner the paradoxical passion of the Reason, while as yet a mere presentiment, retroactively affects man and his self-knowledge so that he who thought to know himself is no longer certain whether he is a more strangely composite animal than

Typhon, or if perchance his nature contains a gentler and diviner part ——.

But what is this unknown something with which the Reason collides when inspired by its paradoxical passion? It is the Unknown. It is not a human being, in so far as we know what man is ; nor is it any other known thing. So let us call this unknown something God.'[1]

We have remarked on the difficulty of interpreting this argument. If we understand Kierkegaard aright he is saying that the process of thought which leads us to the religious assertion is at once rational and extra-rational. In a very peculiar way it leads to the assertion and yet the assertion is different from the reasoning. To put the point differently, Kierkegaard is saying that faith is the answer to a limiting question. Mr. S. Toulmin describes three peculiarities of limiting questions.[2] First, ' our usage provides no standard interpretation of such questions. Then form suggests a meaning of a familiar kind but the situations in which they are asked are such that they cannot have that meaning '. Secondly, the appearance of literalness leads us to expect genuine alternative answers but a limiting question does not present us with genuine alternatives to choose between. ' Finally, a limiting question is not flagrantly " extra-rational " in its form.' This last characteristic is what Kierkegaard had in mind when he talked of the passion of Reason. It is because these questions have not an obviously extra-rational form that we feel impelled to answer them. If we recall our metaphysician in the ethical discussion we can now appreciate that peculiar sense of frustration he has when he is told that there is no point in asking ' Why? ' any more. He feels that this is avoiding the issue, or stopping the argument arbitrarily or putting Reason in a straight-jacket. It is interesting that all these objections have been made against linguistic analysis from time to time, and precisely the same dissatisfaction was felt with Kierkegaard's contention. And yet, surely, the very value of Kierkegaard's remarks is that at least they enable us to understand just what we are doing when we follow Reason right to the limit and want to explore beyond it. The point is that when we have shown that the religious question is like the limiting

---

[1] *Fragments*, pp. 30–1.   [2] op. cit., pp. 205 ff.

question which the metaphysician usually asks when all the reasons have been given, we have said nothing about their impropriety. They are improper only if we see them as literal questions. The difficulty of the religious question is that it does seek information of a peculiar kind. We shall now consider the way a limiting question appears and can appear to be an improper one but actually is the religious question.

Child : ' Mummy, the apples on the tree are held up by the branches, aren't they? '

Mother : ' Yes, David. If the tree were not there they would fall.'

David : ' Why doesn't the tree fall then ? '

Mother : ' Because the earth holds it up. It's just like you and me, the house, anything. Everything is held up by the ground beneath us.'

David : ' I see. (After a pause.) Everything would fall if the earth were not there? '

Mother : ' Well, yes.'

David : ' Mummy, do you know what holds the earth up? '

Mother : ' Well, that's a long story ; but when you are older you'll learn all about it. The earth just holds itself up.'

David : I've been thinking, Mummy, that God holds everything up. I dreamt last night I saw the first tree growing. It was a beautiful tree—just like our apple-blossom. I wanted to know where it came from and I saw an angel and I asked him. He said God had made it and that all the trees in the world were made by God.'

Mother : ' Yes, that's right. That was a beautiful dream.

It is not clear until we come to the end of the story what kind of question David was asking. Now we can go back and say quite definitely he was not asking a nonsensical question. The question was an extension of the quest for reason beyond the limit and was indeed a limiting question. But the child was not misled by the model of ' holding up ' in his beautiful expression of the sense of dependence. When we ask religious questions in the first instance we are driven by the passion of Reason to the point where Reason destroys itself and becomes faith. ' I believe—help thou mine unbelief.'

(v) *The insistence on the inclusion of the person.*

Theodor Haecker has said of the Principle of Subjectivity that it marks the gulf dividing Kierkegaard from the main development of western philosophy.

> ' (It is) the critical point where he shifts the balance, for thought also, from the object to the subject, from the objective world of ideas to the person who has those ideas. It does not meet Kierkegaard's case to say that it all began with Descartes and was carried further by Kant. If there is an analogy at all here, it is of the weakest and most formal kind, and is indeed misleading, since for both Kant and Descartes the self, the subject, is merely an abstract and empty dynamic centre, and all the importance is given to the periphery of the objective system. To Kierkegaard the subject is the concrete and entire person.'[1]

Few people, if any, would deny the truth of this statement.— It is easier, however, to assert it than to describe exactly what we mean when we say that Kierkegaard brought the person of the thinker into philosophy. We shall try to make clear that the statement is true in two different ways, that there are in fact two statements here and not only one. Kierkegaard brought the person into philosophy in the sense that one cannot be said, according to him, to be giving a correct description of religious language if one omits from one's account all reference to feelings, attitudes, hopes and so on. The other sense in which it is true has to do with philosophy itself. This is the claim that philosophy should not be the impersonal ' scientific ' study which it was thought to be. We shall discuss the first sense first.

It had been the prevailing habit of philosophers in the West to regard God as the conclusion of an argument. Whether the argument proceeded from a definition of His existence does not here concern us. The point is that the word ' God ' is thus given a use which is like that of the word ' Binominal Theorem '. Here someone may want to say ' Well what's wrong with this? Presumably, you want to say that God is perfect and so on. But there is nothing incompatible in the definition even if we include what

---

[1] Haecker, *Søren Kierkegaard*, p. 24.

you want to include. . . . Bertrand Russell said something about
the Binominal Theorem being the most beautiful thing in the
world. Any mathematician will tell you that he can see beauty
in mathematics '. The answer is perfectly simple. The term
' Binominal Theorem ' is a term which does not have this emotional connotation to everyone *and need not have it to be understood.*
Whether I see its beauty or not is quite irrelevant to the question
whether I understand it or can prove it. On the other hand, it
is not irrelevant whether I can imagine certain emotional conno-
tations on hearing the word God. Here it may be useful to distinguish between understanding the use of the word ' God '
and using the word correctly oneself. Then it will be true to say
that in order to use the word correctly myself I must have certain
experiences, but to understand its use I need only be able to
imagine what it would be to have these experiences. In his
Systematic Theology Prof. Paul Tillich says that the theologian
must always work within what he calls the theological circle.
The meaning of this term is not altogether clear, but one element
at least is that the theologian must be ' committed ' to the subject
of his discussion, namely God. This is reminiscent too of what
Prof. Farmer tells us so often that one cannot adequately describe
religious faith to one who himself has no faith. It will be clear
that there is some connection between what these two theologians
say and the point with which we are now concerned. Yet there
is also some confusion. For instance, on Tillich's and Farmer's
premises can we call someone a theologian who does not claim
to have any experience such as ' infinite concern ' or ' a sense
of dependence '? The answer would seem to be that we cannot.
Yet, surely there is something odd in saying that A is a brilliant
thinker whose whole life is devoted to the exposition of the classical Christian theology but really is not a theologian. The point
is that we can imagine (even if we do not really know) such a
one and we would be very much inclined to say that there was
no doubt that he was a theologian. Once again, however, we
feel that this statement despite its truth leaves something unsaid
which should be said. It is that we would be tempted to say that
A was not as good a theologian as he could be. Let us imagine
two theologians being discussed by their traditional critics—their
students.

Black : ' I don't think Smith is much of a theologian. We talk about English theology but there's not a single theologian in this University.'

White : ' Well I can't agree that Smith is no theologian, and I think that he and Wilkinson are amongst the best—though they are very different.'

Black : ' Wilkinson—now there's your only hope. He is a brilliant thinker; I've never seen a theologian who could grasp logical points as he can.'

White : ' I grant you that Smith is not as brilliant a logician as Wilkinson but he's got a wonderful sense of what is theologically true.'

Black : ' I've never heard Smith give a lecture in which he doesn't mention " his infinite concern " or " sense of the numinous " or " a feeling of complete dependence and a whole response ". When he talks about the Spirit you can't help feeling that he's about to break out into a " Hallelujah ".'

White : ' Well he doesn't, does he? '

Black : ' No ; it would be better if he did. Then I'd never go to hear him again.'

White : ' But don't you see that he is grasping something Wilkinson never seems to grasp? After all, the Spirit of the living God does mean something to you if you believe in God.'

Black : ' Well, yes. That's true. Perhaps Smith is a better theologian than Wilkinson. But I think Wilkinson is the better thinker, and that's the man you'll learn something from. . . .'

White : ' So long as you agree that Smith is a better theologian I don't care what else you say.'

This point which we have brought out at some length is the intricate point which Kierkegaard makes throughout the *Postscript*. When he relates his parable about the religious pagan and the heathenish Christian[1] and when he affirms ' the possibility of knowing what Christianity is without being a Christian '[2] this is the point he is making. He has an explicit statement of this point in the ' conclusion ' of the *Postscript* where he may be contrasting Martensen with Feuerbach.

'An orthodox champion fights in defence of Christianity

---

[1] op. cit., pp. 179 f.   [2] ibid., p. 332. Cp. p. 331.

M

with the most frightful passion, he protests with the sweat of his brow and with the most concerned demeanour that he accepts Christianity pure and simple, he will live and die in it—and he forgets such expression is an all too general expression for the relation to Christianity —— and he has no inkling of the little ironical secret that a man merely by describing the " how " of his inwardness can show indirectly that he is a Christian without mentioning God's name. —— On the other hand a scoffer attacks Christianity and at the same time expounds it so reliably that it is a pleasure to read him, and one who is in perplexity about finding it distinctly set forth may almost have recourse to him.'[1]

To describe the truth of the claim that Kierkegaard brought the person of the thinker into philosophy is most difficult. It is difficult because it is an extremely subtle thing which, though it appears to repeat the point already made, is quite new. If what we have just said is true, then the philosopher of religion must be able to understand these very complex or sophisticated feelings that we have mentioned. But Kierkegaard's claim is really wider than this. What he said was that the Hegelian philosopher made the mistake of regarding the very life he ' explained ' as something irrelevant to his philosophy and vice versa. He never tired of poking fun at Hegel because of his apparently timeless or other-worldly attitude. This does not strike the average philosopher as funny. One recalls C. D. Broad's famous description of moral philosophy as a game which interests him and people like him but has no connection with moral living. It is our reluctance to abandon this completely that makes Kierkegaard's ' existential-ism ' so difficult for us to understand. Again, it could be argued that he himself never went to the lengths to which later ' existen-tialists ' have gone. For instance, a metaphysic of existence and hope or despair would appear to him to be ridiculous, as indeed it is. He was too much of a rationalist to adopt this way of talking and we shall be well advised to follow him in this. What makes it so difficult to describe his conception of philosophy is that here as always he talked dialectically. Together with his insistence on the propriety and value of metaphysics we have the clear emphasis on subjectivity and the importance of the person.

[1] ibid., pp. 542–3.

Nowadays we are very prone indeed to regard the divorce between philosophy and life against which Kierkegaard protested as being the only proper state of affairs. This has been described by the late R. G. Collingwood in his *Autobiography*; and his description deserves quotation :

> ' The school of Green had taught that philosophy was not a preserve for professional philosophers, but everyone's business ; and the pupils of this school had gradually formed a block of opinion in the country whose members, though not professional philosophers, were interested in the subject, regarding it as important. . . . As these men died, no one took their place ; and by about 1920 I found myself asking " Why is it that nowadays no Oxford man, unless he is either about 70 years old or else a teacher of philosophy—regards philosophy as anything but a futile parlour game? " The answer was not difficult to find, and was confirmed by the fact that the " realists " unlike the school of Green, did think philosophy a preserve for professional philosophers. The fox was tailless, and knew it. But this mental kind of audition, when people part with their morals, their religion, the learning they acquired at school and so forth, is commonly regarded by the tailless as an improvement in their condition ; and so it was with the " realists ". —— They were proud to have excogitated a philosophy so pure from the sordid taint of utility that they could lay their hands on their hearts and say it was no use at all.'[1]

For Kierkegaard this divorce of philosophy and life was a betrayal of the legacy Socrates had given to philosophy. In Socrates he saw the figure of the ' subjective ' philosopher the man whose philosophy was not a futile parlour game but the very essence of his life. Philosophy, says Kierkegaard, must be the building in which a man lives or it is nothing. The problem is indeed how to achieve this without glossing over the difference between the philosophy and the concrete reality. The answer may be that by taking note of the living quality of the things we are discussing we shall be not only better philosophers but wiser men. But whatever the answer is, Kierkegaard makes an important

---

[1] *Collingwood*, op. cit., pp. 50-1.

contribution by reminding us of the need to make philosophy more concerned with living than it has been of late.

(vi) *The clue to the meaningfulness of religion.*

All that we have said so far could be summed up in an epigrammatic way by saying that Kierkegaard has done philosophy of religion immense service by showing us the possibility of regarding religion as meaningful discourse. We approached this study of Kierkegaard's work with the conviction that he could give us a clue in our attempt to understand the central puzzles of the philosophy of religion. We looked to him for help because he made it his business to give us an exact account of what Christian faith consisted in and what relation there was between this attitude and the philosopher's quest. His work has become a part of the great tradition of Christian literature, an expression of a man's profoundest belief and commitment. This is not to say that Kierkegaard's sole importance is as an author of pious literature. On the contrary, his criticism of the way faith had been understood by the contemporary philosophers and theologians has a great importance for us because this question of the nature of faith is the problem which engrosses every philosophical theologian's interest. Theologians have been bewildered by the treatment of religious language by the linguistic philosophers. The difficulty they have felt is that they do not know how to reply to what they take to be a severe criticism. What we have been trying to bring out in our examination of what Kierkegaard meant by faith is that the assertions of such a Christian thinker can be understood best by means of the technique these philosophers use. So understood they provide material for a reply to any denial of the meaningfulness of religious language. We have seen that Kierkegaard's understanding of faith was a very complex matter, and that, despite the simplicity of the slogan, the Principle of Subjectivity has more than one meaning or use. One of its most important uses was as a refutation of the idea that faith was somehow as simple and objective a matter as proof taken either in the sense of a logical demonstration or verification of a scientific hypothesis. That faith can be described as a logical demonstration it is quite ridiculous to suggest. However, the assumption that it should be capable of such strict demonstration dies very hard. But we have seen that this too is impossible for two very good reasons. The one is that no existential statement can be logically demonstrated and the other is that the attitude of faith precludes the possibility that its object can be proved. It is therefore wrong to say that it is the business of philosophy of religion to make faith reasonable in the sense of giving faith the demonstration of its truth which as it were it does not carry within itself. The business of philosophy of religion is to describe the religious man's faith and show us its place on the map of language which philosophy traces. In this way it does have a great deal to do with showing the *objectivity* of faith. We have seen the analogy between the objectivity of religious faith and that of ethics. Where it differs radically from the logic of ethics is in the necessity of the existential claim to faith. How do we come to make this claim? The first point that we can make by way of reply is that certain experiences lead us to the belief in God. These experiences are of two different types—the one may be called cosmological and the other quasi-ethical. The former is the experience of the world as one whole which somehow leaves us with a sense of mystery that is only half-explained when all the explanations have been given. This is the limiting question logic that we have partly described already. We can go back to this quite briefly again and notice how it is true of all the great religious thinkers that they have recognised the connection between this experience of the world and our belief in God. Augustine expresses it better than anyone.

' I asked the earth and it answered me " I am not He ", and whatsoever are in it confessed the same. I asked the sea and the deeps and the living creeping things, and they answered " We are not thy God, seek above us." I asked the moving air; and the whole air with its inhabitants answers "Anaximenes was deceived. I am not God". I asked the heavens, sun and moon and stars; " Nor " answered they " are we the God whom thou seekest ". And I replied unto all the things which encompass the door of my flesh : " Ye have told me of my God, that ye are not He, tell me something of him ". And they cried out with a loud voice " He made us " —— I asked the whole frame of the world about my God ; and it answered me " I am not He, but He made me ".[1]

St. Thomas expressed the very same attitude in his argument from contingency, and both Hume and Kant speak of the power of this kind of argument. It is, of course, difficult to describe the meaning of this word contingency here with any sort of logical exactitude. The assertion that the world is contingent is a tautology if we are using the word contingent in its logical sense. But clearly we are putting forward a synthetic statement here, saying something new or strange about the world. ' The world does not explain itself ', we say ; and nothing is further from our minds than the need for any more explanations to be provided by the scientist. For this reason it is wrong to say that there are good grounds or sufficient reasons for believing in God. We do not reach the theistic position by arguing from any evidences. How can you get from the historical to the eternal? asks Kierkegaard. And his answer is that you have to jump, you have to make the leap.

The second kind of experience the quasi-ethical, is the experience of sin and guilt. For Kierkegaard there is only one reason why anyone should accept the infinite self-made care of faith, and the reason is the consciousness of guilt. Thus he says :

> ' There is only one proof of the birth of Christianity and that, quite rightly, is from the emotions, when the dread of sin and a heavy conscience torture a man into crossing the narrow line between despair bordering upon madness and Christianity.'[2]

This second experience is what shatters the ' immediate faith ' which he scorns. To the man who regards God's existence as one of those unquestioned assumptions which make up the furniture of everyone's mental home, the consciousness of *sin* comes as a rude awakening. The concept gains a dynamic ethical significance and is seen to indicate the Person against whom he has sinned. In such a situation we see that the relationship between us and God is not the unquestioned thing we thought

---

[1] Augustine, *Confessions*, Bk. X, vi, 9.   [2] *Journals*, 314.

it was. The dread of sin has made us aware of God as our salvation. The guilt which oppresses us makes us aware of God who
is our Judge. The importance of this second kind of experience
is two-fold. It is logically dependent on the first in that we cannot
be conscious of sin without some conception of God such as
we have in the Christian doctrines of Creation. Thus for Kierkegaard man is a synthesis of infinity and finitude, of eternity and
temporality. Despair, he says, is the misrelation in the relation
of the self to itself. Kierkegaard claims that this disease of despair
is universal, that not even the most convinced Christian can avoid
sometimes being ' somewhat in despair '. In *The Sickness Unto
Death* and *The Concept of Dread* he has given us the most important
modern description of sin. When one has experienced despair
in fear and trembling one turns to the mysterious invitation of the
majestic Lowly One who says ' Come unto me '. The second
important aspect of this experience is now clear : the religious
attitude is born of certain experiences and is meant to constitute
a policy of action in the face of these experiences. This is the
' existential ' aspect of faith which Kierkegaard has described for
us. If we can hazard a paradox of our own to describe Kierkegaard's dialectical account of religion we can say that faith is an
attitude which is interested in what is outside itself but is born of
experiences and has a close relation to such experiences. Faith is
holding fast the uncertain in passionate certitude, staking my all
on the God of my salvation, Who delivers me from the bondage
of despair.

That Kierkegaard appreciated the importance of the existential
claim which religious faith makes is clear, but it is not quite as
clear how he interprets it. Thus, having said that faith is born
of these experiences he says very little that can be easily construed
about the problem of logical justification which must arise.
Granted the attitude of faith, what answer is to be given to the
man who asks whether the attitude is justified? Kierkegaard
wrongly assumed that anyone who asks this question has no
interest in faith or at any rate too often speaks in such a way as
to suggest this. If I know that a lion has escaped from the circus
that has come to town I shall be very careful to be on the look-out
for anything like a lion. Should I see the lion I shall probably
run far enough away from it. We would say that this attitude is

very justified because lions are not creatures to be regarded as pets, and this lion had already killed the trainer and so on. Now it is not at once clear that the religious situation has the same definite justification. The danger is that of thinking that since this kind of justification is not present then there is no justification possible. This results in the view that religious assertions are either false or indeed meaningless and nonsensical. In fact the most characteristic note in the whole melody of philosophy of religion is the sounding of this dilemma. A great many writers are agreed on one thing : that linguistic empiricism constitutes a threat to the theologian's claim that religious assertions are meaningful and true. Of course, some forms of this empiricism do deny that religious assertions have meaning. But this is only because they make ' meaning ' a univocal term and expect religious assertions to have the same kind of meaning as scientific assertions. We have seen that faith is not scientific proof. The question is then whether faith has any other kind of meaning and what would be its justification. Here we get enlightenment from Kierkegaard despite himself. The tendency to irrationalism which we saw in his idea of subjectivity made him regard faith as something opposed to any rational belief. He was dominated by the popular models of mathematics and science. However, he was a great enough thinker to break through the domination to an understanding of the very point he seemed to deny. The meaning of faith's assertion is to be found in the complex of statements about an awareness which we have in some situations and statements about our dispositions, attitudes and intentions. It is the priority of the awareness that renders it impossible to translate statements about belief into psychological statements or ethical statements. The attitudes that we have described have been seen to contain the concept of God already. The belief in God is not an inference from certain information about the world. The weakness of the traditional cosmological argument was that it made faith rest on certain evidence and in this way it distorted faith. Kierkegaard was thus right in saying that traditional theistic arguments made belief a calculation of probability. However, he was too hasty in his assumption that because faith was the result of choice its certitude must be psychological. He himself grasped the peculiarly rational character of the extra-rational certainty in faith's 'I know that my Redeemer liveth'. We have been at pains to bring out both these points more clearly than he himself does—not indeed more powerfully but simply less ambiguously. If we are to see the meaning of religious assertions then we must carefully consider those attitudes and policy statements that we have seen in it. The only question we shall deal with here is the formal one of the way in which these statements have meaning. In his essay on 'Language Strata'[1] Dr. F. Waissman speaks of I-sentences as expressing end-points of verification, these end-points being experiences in which 'Knowledge comes into direct contact with reality'. It is in this margin of all verification that we shall find the sort of meaning which religious statements have and the truth which is subjectivity. They are in fact like three different situations and their meaning is as it were an amalgam of these three kinds of meaning. Let us consider these three different situations.

A.

Master : 'The angles of a triangle make up one hundred and eighty degrees. Jones minor, will you demonstrate this theorem.'

Jones minor tries and fails. He just has no idea how to do the problem and in the end confesses this. The master goes through the theorem step by step and then asks 'Now can you do it?' The boy tries again, and again he fails. If after this procedure has been followed twice or three times the boy finally grasps the theorem, he will say 'Yes I see now'.

B.

Smith : 'You know, I've been thinking a lot lately about the people in the poor districts of our town.

Jones : 'Well yes I've thought of them too. But what's the use?'

Smith : 'That's it. I've told myself that it's no use, but something keeps disturbing me.'

Jones : I see no reason why you should be disturbed because people reap the bitter harvest of their folly.

Smith : 'Harvest of their own folly may be right. But I am going to devote my life to these people and I shall try to help

---

[1] *Logic and Language* (ed. Flew), Second Series, p. 25. Blackwell, Oxford, 1953.

them better their lot by being one of them and giving them a hand.'[1]

C.

Black : ' I think Albert Schweitzer is the most wonderful man I know alive.'

White : ' I don't see why you admire him so much.'

Black : ' Just think of what he has done.'

White : ' He's not achieved all that much has he? I'm told he is not such a wonderful organist and as far as his hospital goes it is almost useless.'

Black : ' That is not the point. He may be a good organist and a good doctor or he may not be. The point is that he is a good, a supremely good man. Think of sacrificing a prominent place in Europe to go to the lonely shores of Africa to serve his fellow-man.'

White : ' Well, I agree. You're right there. He made a noble sacrifice and he is very much to be admired.'

These three situations can all be compared with the religious situation, and the logic of each helps us to understand the logic of religious language. Let us take the first example, the boy who is being taught mathematics. What is of great interest to us here is the boy's remark ' I see '. How are we to understand this? Is he simply saying that he can now work through the problem? It is true that if we wanted to check on the success of this lesson in mathematics, we would have to see whether he could do the problem or not. But this is not the same as saying that the boy's remark *means* no more than this. And indeed it is perfectly clear that the boy is describing something which has happened to him. There are many ways in which we could describe it—for instance ' It came to me all at once ', ' I suddenly saw the way it came out '. What is important is that all these statements reveal an end-point of verification. Their content cannot then be exhausted by analysis in terms of public language. Unless the boy says ' I see ' or something like it the lesson is a failure. There is an obvious similarity between this and the religious man's ' I know ' or ' I

---

[1] An example of this kind of policy-decision is Sally's story in Mr. Howard Spring's *The Houses in Between* ; different, but similar in the essential point of decision, are the stories of St. Francis of Assisi and that of Albert Schweitzer's decision to become a missionary in darkest Africa.

believe '. Kierkegaard's central point about subjectivity might be described as the emphasis on the fact that 'I' was an ineradicable element of any religious statement. These statements have a different logic from that of the public statements where 'I' is eradicable. They demand in fact ' the logic of personality '. This is difficult to describe and we can only hazard a brief observation about what is relevant here. Since this logic is that of language whose purpose it is to express and describe certain experiences it cannot be fully analysed in terms of what is publicly verifiable. This would be to make the subjective objective, which Kierkegaard regarded as the besetting sin of the theologian. It follows then that no description of these experiences can validate the apparently public or ontological claim of religious faith. But whilst these experiences are not evidence for the assertion that God exists and cannot be said to justify the religious man's claim that he knows God, yet it is equally certain that they are an essential part of the statement. That is, the religious man's statement is not a bare ontological claim but a statement that is at once ontological and autobiographical. The ontology and autobiography are related, so that to say that I believe God exists *means* that I worship Him. Here we see the resemblance to situation C where the admission that Schweitzer is a good man implies that he is to be admired. Further, the ethical implication of the claim that God exists is like situation B where the existence of poor people implies a policy decision. If I confess my faith in God I am confessing that He is the policy on which I decide, the way of life I accept. ' Be ye perfect ' said Jesus Christ ' *because* your Father in Heaven is perfect '.

The justification of religious faith has always been said by the saints to lie within itself. This is true then logically as well as psychologically. It is not only that I am confirmed in my belief by my experience. The experience contains the concept representing the object of my belief. It is thus the only proper and true attitude. It will be said perhaps that this is to empty faith of its significance. But to say this carries us back to the demand that faith should have the same kind of meaning as publicly verifiable statements. And this is to ask for the impossible. In the same way Kierkegaard has shown that asking for a logically simple doctrine of Incarnation is to demand what the Christian cannot

172 *Subjectivity and Paradox*

give. The doctrine of Incarnation describes the significance of the Person of Jesus Christ. Kierkegaard held fast to the faith that declares the Nazarene the Lord and Saviour. In his passionate concern to describe this faith correctly and fully he spoke of it as faith in the Paradox. How has this helped us? It has helped us first to grasp the logical peculiarity of the statement : ' Jesus Christ is God '. It has been an expression of a point that some theologians are now making in a different way. Bultmann's myth is very much like Kierkegaard's contradiction. Neither is literally true. If we examine the logic of the Christological statement we shall see (as we have seen) that it uses the same subject for a historical statement and a non-historical one. This logical impropriety is the very source of the religious use of this state-ment. It is not my ultimate concern to know how it is possible to make these two statements both true. The question is not ' What is the analysis of the Christ-statement? ' The question is ' What think ye of Christ? '. ' Who say ye that I am? ' is the question He always asks the believer. The important thing is not understanding the Paradox—that is impossible : it is rather to believe that Jesus Christ is the revelation of God Himself, the dawning of the new age, the salvation of all men, the pattern of my life.

The road we have travelled has been a very winding one, and has taken us through many mires and over much rough ground. The guide we chose has proved faithful. He reached the heights of understanding in his own unswerving allegiance to God. In living the faith he understood it. His work remains a monument to the memory of a great Christian life. He never asked for disciples. Our study has not been pursued in any spirit of hero-worship or of a ' parrot-like echo '. Kierkegaard has his weaknesses—the chief of which being that he never was content to state a point without exaggerating it. But it is abundantly clear that his work is a valuable contribution to Philosophy of Religion in two ways. The first is that we see the complexity of the logic of religious statements in the dialectical way in which he describes faith. The other lesson he has taught us is that the important thing is to live the faith. Faith is living or it is nothing. To understand these two lessons fully is something his poet or ' the individual ' will do. If we have been able to point the way we shall have done him the service we owe him.

A BIBLIOGRAPHY OF ENGLISH KIERKEGAARDIANA

I. First, there are the excellent translations of most of Kierkegaard's writings, for which we are indebted to Swenson, Lowrie and Dru. Swenson and Lowrie have translated the works, and Major Dru a selection from the Journal. All these are published by the Oxford University Press.

II. WORKS ON KIERKEGAARD

1. Allen, E. L., *Kierkegaard, His Life and Thought*, London, 1935.
   One of the earliest works published in England. It is a good introductory work, but is of little value today.
2. Bain, J. A., *Søren Kierkegaard, His Life and Religious Teaching*, London, 1935.
   This is another interesting account of Kierkegaard's life and work which is now mainly of antiquarian interest.
3. Bonifazi, C., *Christendom Attacked*, Rockliff, London, 1953.
   An interesting, brief comparison of the understanding of Christianity in the work of Kierkegaard and Nietzche.
4. Casserley, J. V. L., *The Christian in Philosophy*, pp. 150–182, Faber and Faber, London, 1949.
   This has been called the best introduction to Kierkegaard in English. It hardly merits this description, being a compact but sketchy account of Kierkegaard's thought.
5. Channing-Pearce, M., *The Terrible Crystal*, London, Kegan Paul, 1940.
6. Channing-Pearce, M., *Søren Kierkegaard*, London, 1945.
   Both these works are popular studies which are interesting and well-written but hardly important.
7. Collins, J., *The Mind of Kierkegaard*, Chicago, 1953.
   This has been well received in America. It is to appear in Britain too.
8. Croxall, T. H., *Kierkegaard Studies*, London, Lutterworth Press, 1948.
   A useful discussion of Kierkegaard's philosophy, aesthetics and religious views. It does not always cut deep enough.
9. De Lubac, H., *The Drama of Atheistic Humanism*, London, 1949.
   This does not give any real information about Kierkegaard or any explanation.
10. Fulford, F. W., *Sören Aabye Kierkegaard, A Study*, Cambridge, 1911.
    This is the earliest English book on Kierkegaard and is a very good discussion of his thought on the then available data.
11. Geismar, E., *Lectures on the Religious Thought of Kierkegaard*, Minneapolis, U.S.A., 1937.
    This is the one book in English by the greatest Kierkegaard scholar of the century. It is a profound study of his ' theology '.
12. Haecker, T., *Søren Kierkegaard*, Oxford, 1937.
    A sensitive appreciation of Kierkegaard's place in the history of philosophy.
13. Haecker, T., *Kierkegaard the Cripple*, London, 1948.
    An attempt to discover the nature of Kierkegaard's physical deformity.
14. Hohlenberg, J., *Sören Kierkegaard*, London, 1954.
    A fascinating study of a hero. Somewhat speculative but useful for background.
15. Henriksen, A., *Methods and Results of Kierkegaard Studies in Scandinavia*, Copenhagen, 1950.
    An extremely valuable history of the literature published on Kierkegaard in Scandinavia.
16. Jolivet, R., *Introduction to Kierkegaard*, Muller, London, 1950.
    This is a useful introduction, presenting Kierkegaard's thought clearly.

17. Lowrie, W., *Kierkegaard*, Oxford, 1938.
This remains the most important book on Kierkegaard. It is indispensable both as a biography and as an exposition of his thought.
18. Mackintosh, H. R., *Types of Modern Theology*, pp. 218–262, Nisbet, London, 1937.
An excellent brief summary of Kierkegaard's religious thought.
19. Martin, H. V., *The Prophet of the Absolute*, Madras, 1942.
A slight book on the absoluteness of Kierkegaarde's message.
20. Martin, H. V., *Søren Kierkegaard, The Melancholy Dane*, Epworth Press, London, 1950.
A very readable introduction to Kierkegaard's life and work. It covers most of the ground in an elementary but sound way.
21. Martin, H. V., *The Wings of Faith*, Epworth Press, London, 1950.
A discussion of Kierkegaard's views on the nature of faith which, though useful, does not make any contribution to Kierkegaard study.
22. Patrick, D. G. M., *Pascal and Kierkegaard*, Vol. 2, Lutterworth Press, London, 1948.
This is a thorough exposition of all Kierkegaard's work from an apologetic point of view.
23. Swenson, D. F., *Something about Kierkegaard*, Minneapolis, U.S.A., 1945.
This is the best brief study of Kierkegaard in English written by a famous Kierkegaard translator and scholar.
24. Wyschogrod, M., *Kierkegaard and Heidegger*, Kegan Paul, London, 1954.
A study of two existentialist ontologies. It is often stimulating, but on the whole is not a reliable exposition of Kierkegaard.

III. ARTICLES.
There are a number of very useful articles on Kierkegaard in English published in such journals as *Philosophy*, *Scottish Journal of Theology*, *The Hibbert Journal*, etc.